The Fresh Bartender's

Guide To
Healthy Parties and

Festive Juicing

Jordan Maerin

Pure Energy Publishing
Seattle, Washington

ISBN-13: 978-0-9774858-4-0
First Edition, 2009
Printed in the USA

Published by
Pure Energy Publishing, Seattle, Washington
www.pureenergypub.com

Disclaimer:
The responsibility for any miraculously rejuvenating or adverse detoxification effects or consequences resulting from the use of any suggestions described hereafter lies not with the author or distributors of this book. This book is not intended as medical advice. By following any dietary program, you are prescribing for yourself, which is your right.

Contents

Special Ingredients

THE FRESH BARTENDER

This book is dedicated to
the memory of Brian Anderson.
You had fun in spite of yourself.

Acknowledgements

I send hearty thanks to all of my fellow bartenders over the years; it's no wonder we got along so well - you're a scrappy, hyper and nocturnal bunch.

Thanks to the staff of Nature's First Law 2004-2006 for showing me how celebratory healthy foods can be and how easy it is to create miracles when we live, love and eat consciously.

Thanks also to Anna Bielecki for your infinite support and inspiration - we've been cohorts in creating a healthy balance between flavor and health within the restaurant industry.

And thanks to LaDawn for your love and faith - you inspire the best in me.

"Get the Party started!"

THE FRESH BARTENDER

Introduction

*"I would rather entertain and hope that people
learned something than educate people and
hope they were entertained." - Walt Disney*

Would you serve a smoothie at a party? You *will* once you start using this book – but you won't call it a smoothie. You'll give it an exotic name and serve it in a fancy glass with a colorful parasol, with festive music setting the mood.

This book is about **luxury and health** (yes, I said those two words in the same sentence!). The Fresh Party of the future is one that brings everyone together. It combines the electrifying flavors *and* the health benefits of fresh juices in an atmosphere that's festive, loving and celebratory.

This book will teach you how to spoil yourself and your Fresh Party guests, all in the name of good cheer and fun. After all, it's only the highest-end, most luxurious spas and resorts in the world that serve *fresh* exotic juices at a traditional style bar, in a social atmosphere.

The time is ripe for innovative Fresh Bartenders to heal the rift between "tasty" and "good for you." I think a Fresh Party is just what the doctor ordered, and this book is your prescription.

Veggie Tray Outcasts

This book is for anyone who's ever hovered over the veggie tray at a party (the one you brought!) while everyone else gorges on junk food. It's for people who avoid parties because they don't want to be tempted by foods that will only bring them down later. It's for anyone who eats at coffee shops because the social atmosphere is so vital. It's for everyone who avoids healthier diets altogether because they don't want to ditch their current friends for new ones. And it's for those friends of ours who would throw us healthier parties, if they only knew how.

Are health food diets inherently anti-social? Do they invariably make non-dieters defensive? Not any more! It's time for "health nuts" to start throwing our own parties, in a casual atmosphere where everyone can enjoy themselves to the max!

A Fresh Cocktail Party

I have focused on beverages in this party book (rather than on food) for several reasons:

- Everyone can enjoy fresh juices for fun, no matter what they're eating for dinner.

- A "cocktail party" is more casual for your guests, and less labor-intensive for you, than a dinner party.

- There will be no hard feelings because your guests found the health food meal you prepared too light or unfamiliar.

- A juice party works just as well in the middle of the day as it does after dinnertime.

- It can be tailored to kids as well as adults.

- It's a light-hearted way to introduce **new traditions** to your circle of family and friends. See Chapter 6 for ideas about Fresh Party occasions and themes.

- Throwing a Fresh Party will keep you focused on what really makes a party successful: love, intention and **atmosphere!** The rest is just details.

It's All In The Presentation

Creating a Fresh Party is all about atmosphere and presentation, and fancy glasses and garnishes are your most important tools for turning ordinary drinks into exotic cocktails.

Bar glasses can be purchased online and at restaurant supply stores. You can also find them at many resale shops, and even garage sales and flea markets. You could collect souvenir glasses from around the world that have been ditched at resale venues. See Appendix III for the specific glasses used in this book.

Colorful garnishes can range from simple pitted cherries and berries to large chunks of pineapple and melon. Citrus fruits can be cut into twists, wedges and wheels. Present several cherries, berries or grapes on a plastic sword, or add a paper parasol for a tropical or feminine flair. See the photos on the following page.

Finally, setting up your Fresh Bar like a pro will help your guests feel festive and well taken care of. See Appendix III for complete details.

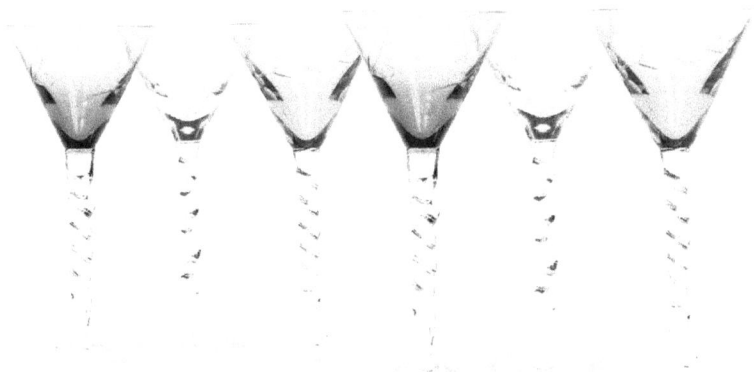

See Appendix III for the glasses used in this book

Fresh Garnishes

Wheel
Use citrus, kiwi or a banana chunk with the peel. Cut it thicker to anchor a parasol.

Slice
A half wheel is more appropriate for smaller glasses.

Wedge
This one's utilitarian - great for an extra squirt of citrus.

Pineapple Wedge
A tropical classic that can anchor a parasol.

Pick or Sword
For playful dunking of berries and grapes.

Parasol/Strawberry
You may need a small fruit to hold it open and a large fruit to anchor it.

Sprig of Mint
Perfect for hot summer days.

The Art of the Twist - Cut the peel of a lemon or lime into strips as shown above. Each strip should be twisted over the beverage to release the oil and then rubbed all around the rim of the glass for flavor.

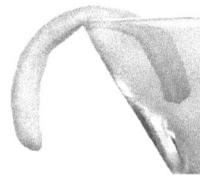

How It Works

Minimal equipment needed. First, a citrus juicer (manual or electric), and second, a blender for slushes and nut creams.

Chill It! Your beverages should have strong flavors, so prevent ice melting into them by keeping your fruit and juices cold.

Chilling glassware with ice or ice water is recommended when straining drinks "straight up" into martini, cocktail or wine glasses.

Shake it! Shaking beverages with ice is great for chilling and blending of flavors, sweeteners and nut creams. Any cup with a secure lid will work, or purchase a bar shaker (see Appendix III).

"Do I have to shake the drinks?" No, just stir in the agave syrup well and add an emulsifier to your nut creams (see page 50).

Make large batches. Make pitchers of drinks to save time; the volume equivalents below will help you multiply the ingredients.

Volume Equivalents

1 teaspoon = 1/8 ounce

1 Tablespoon = 3/8 ounce

½ Jigger = 2 Tablespoons = ¾ ounce

1 "Splash" = 1 Pony = 1 ounce

1 Jigger = 4 Tablespoons = 1 ½ ounces

1 cup = 8 ounces

2 quarts = 8 cups = 64 ounces

1 gallon = 16 cups = 128 ounces

Note: All equivalents listed are for *fluid ounces*, not ounces of weight. Ounces of weight will have a grams equivalent on the label, as with Madhava agave syrup. There is no direct correlation between fluid ounces and ounces of weight across different substances.

The School of Fresh

Keep your first Fresh Parties small and manageable - after all, you want to have fun too! Here are some tips for throwing exactly the kind of Fresh Party that's right for you:

Freshman
- 2 to 4 guests is plenty.
- Multiply a recipe out and make a whole pitcher ahead of time.
- Allow for one additional option for your guests, e.g. create a pitcher of Apple Sour and offer ginger juice as an option.
- Serve simple fresh fruit and nuts, or make it a potluck.

Sophomore
- 4 to 8 guests is manageable.
- Make juices and nut creams ahead of time and keep chilled until serving.
- Have a few drink options, using different combinations of the same juices, or two different drinks with shaken and blended options.

Junior
- You can handle 8 to 16 guests by now.
- Throw a Fresh Theme Party in order to keep your offerings manageable and well organized - use the suggestions in Chapter 6 to create a drink and snack menu.

Senior
- Offer multiple drink options and do some fresh juicing of chilled fruit.
- Show off with that shaker!
- Enlist some helpers, if necessary, to make some gourmet snacks; eventually, you can train fellow Fresh Bartenders to help you throw bigger Fresh Parties.

Chapter 1
Juices & Herbal Teas

"You only live once, but if you do it right, once is enough." - Mae West

When making drinks for a Fresh Party, your focus should be on two things: creating a festive mood, and concocting beverages that are strongly flavored.

You can create a festive mood in several ways: by using fancy glassware and colorful garnishes; by creating a festive environment with music and decor; and by adding visual and auditory excitement by using your *shaker* to mix beverages. See Appendix III for glasses and bar equipment; the Introduction for garnishes; and Chapter 6 for Theme Party decor ideas.

Concocting strongly flavored beverages is vital for a Fresh Party because you want your guests to stay for a while and sip their drinks. These drinks will be sweeter, more sour and richer than the smoothies you make before going to the gym. The recipes in this book are meant to be strongly flavored, and the smaller the glass, the more strongly flavored or richer it should be.

The other way to keep your drinks strong is to make sure your fruit, juices and creams are chilled before using, so they won't cause the ice to melt quickly and water down the beverage.

Real Bloody Mary

¾ cup (6 oz) fresh ripe Tomato Juice

Juice of 1 stalk Celery

1 Tbsp Lemon Juice

2 tsp Nama Shoyu or Tamari or Worcestershire Sauce

Sprinkle each of Cayenne, Sea Salt and Black Pepper

Put all ingredients in a hurricane glass and stir together. Fill with ice and garnish with a celery stick and a lime wedge.

Bloody Caesar: add ½ tsp of dulse or kelp flakes.

🍷 Sunrise Margarita

¾ cup (6 oz) Orange Juice

¼ cup (2 oz) Lemon Juice

¼ cup (2 oz) Lime Juice

16 counts (¼ cup) Agave Syrup

Stir, shake or blend with 2 cups of ice and serve in a hurricane glass. Garnish with a lime wheel. Rim with margarita salt, if desired.

Agave Syrup

Agave syrup is a *must* for your Fresh Bar, for two reasons. First, because it's a natural sweetener with a non-invasive flavor. And second, because it's a liquid, so it will dissolve easily in cold beverages. A raw, unprocessed honey would be a good second choice, but pure maple syrup tends to have a more distinctive, invasive flavor.

The amount of agave syrup may vary based on the ripeness and type of the fruit you use. For instance, drinks with riper pineapple and banana, and sweeter apples, will require less agave than these recipes call for.

Measuring agave syrup is messy because it's so sticky, so for individual drinks, I use *count measures* instead of spoon measures. Simply keep your agave syrup in a squeeze bottle with a ¼ -inch opening and count the length of time you squirt the agave into the beverage using light pressure.

1 count Agave Syrup = A one-second squirt

16 counts = ¼ cup

🍸 Deep Forest Freeze

1 cup Orange Juice

1 cup Mixed Berries, frozen

1 ripe Banana

8 counts Agave Syrup

Blend with 1 cup of ice and serve in a hurricane glass. Garnish with an orange wheel.

🍸 Fruity Freeze

¾ cup (6 oz) Orange Juice

¼ cup (2 oz) Lemon or Lime Juice

½ cup Melon chunks

1 whole Kiwi

10 counts Agave Syrup

Blend with 1 ½ cups of ice and serve in a hurricane glass. Garnish with an orange wheel.

🍸 Poolside Freeze

1 cup Orange Juice

Splash (1 oz) Lime Juice

½ cup Honeydew Melon chunks

½ cup Peach slices, frozen

10 counts Agave Syrup

Blend with 1 ½ cups of ice and serve in a hurricane glass. Garnish with an orange wheel.

Peach Daiquiri

1 COUNT
aGaVe SYRUP
= a 1-second
SQUIRT
see page 15

¾ cup (6 oz) Orange Juice

¼ cup (2 oz) Lemon Juice

1 cup Peach slices, frozen

10 counts Agave Syrup

Blend with 1 cup of ice and serve in a hurricane glass. Garnish with a lime wheel.

Harvest Time

½ cup (4 oz) Apple Juice

¼ cup (2 oz) Orange Juice

Splash (1 oz) Lime Juice

1 ripe Banana

½ cup Apple slices, frozen or fresh

12 counts Agave Syrup, or less if using sweet apples

Blend with 1 ½ cups of ice and serve in a hurricane glass. Garnish with an orange wheel.

Sour Apple

1/3 cup (3 oz) Apple Juice

2 Tbsp (¾ oz) Lime Juice

2 Tbsp (¾ oz) Lemon Juice

6 counts Agave Syrup, or less if using sweet apples

Stir and chill or shake with ice, and strain into a chilled cocktail glass.

Apple Jack

½ cup (4 oz) Apple Juice

Splash (1 oz) Pineapple Juice

Splash (1 oz) Lemon Juice

4 counts Agave Syrup, or less if using sweet apples

Shake with 1 cup of ice, or stir then add ice. Serve in a highball glass with a pineapple wedge or lime slice.

Ginger Apple Sour

½ cup (4 oz) Apple Juice

¼ cup (2 oz) Lemon Juice

½ Tbsp Ginger Juice

8 counts Agave Syrup, or less if using sweet apples

Shake with 1 cup of ice, or stir then add ice. Serve in a highball glass with a lemon wedge.

Fresh Ginger

For a distinctive, stimulating flavor "kick," nothing beats fresh ginger! In a blended drink made with a heavy duty blender, you can simply add a chunk of peeled ginger. Otherwise, you can finely grate your ginger by hand, adding some of the pulp directly to the drink or squeezing the juice out and discarding the dry pulp left over.

18

Melon Margarita

1 COUNT AGAVE SYRUP = a 1-second SQUIRT see page 15

¾ cup (6 oz) Orange Juice

¼ cup (2 oz) Lime Juice

1 cup Honeydew Melon chunks

10 counts Agave Syrup

Blend with 1 ½ cups of ice and serve in a hurricane glass. Garnish with a lime slice.

Green Bay Smash

¾ cup (6 oz) Pineapple Juice

¼ cup (2 oz) Orange Juice

½ cup Honeydew Melon chunks

1 ripe Banana

8 counts Agave Syrup

Blend with 1 ½ cups of ice and serve in a hurricane glass. Garnish with a pineapple wedge or an orange wheel.

Honeydew Cocktail

¼ cup (2 oz) Honeydew Melon Juice

Splash (1 oz) Pineapple Juice

Splash (1 oz) Lime Juice

3 counts Agave Syrup

Stir and chill or shake with ice, and strain into a chilled cocktail glass. Garnish with a lime twist.

Sunrise in Paradise

Honeydew Melon pieces, muddled

½ cup (4 oz) Honeydew Melon Juice

Splash (1 oz) Orange Juice

Splash (1 oz) Lemon Juice

2 counts Agave Syrup

Muddler
See Appendix III

Muddle a few chunks of ripe honeydew in a highball or other thick-bottomed glass. Shake the rest with 1 cup of ice, or stir then add ice. Garnish with an orange wheel.

Strawberry Bash

1 cup (8 oz) Pineapple or Orange Juice

1 cup Strawberries, frozen

1 ripe Banana

8 counts Agave Syrup

Blend with 1 cup of ice and serve in a hurricane glass. Garnish with a fresh strawberry or an orange wheel.

Bayou Sunset

1 cup Orange Juice

½ cup Black Raspberries or Cherries, frozen

½ cup Peach slices, frozen

10 counts Agave Syrup

Blend with 1 cup of ice and serve in a hurricane glass. Garnish with an orange wheel.

THE FRESH BARTENDER

Pacific Islander

1 count agave syrup = a 1-second squirt
see page 15

½ cup (4 oz) each Pineapple & Orange Juice

½ cup Black Raspberries or Cherries, frozen

1 ripe Banana

8 counts Agave Syrup

Blend with 1 ½ cups of ice and serve in a hurricane glass. Garnish with a pineapple wedge.

Tropical Sunrise

1 cup Orange Juice

½ cup Pineapple chunks, fresh or frozen

½ cup Mango chunks, fresh or frozen

½ Banana

10 counts Agave Syrup

Blend with 1 ½ cups of ice and serve in a hurricane glass. Garnish with an orange wheel.

Tree Climber

2 slices ripe Pear

½ cup (4 oz) Apple Juice

Splash (1 oz) Lime Juice

2 Tbsp (¾ oz) Pure Cranberry Juice

12 counts Agave Syrup, or less if using sweet apples

Muddle 2 slices of pear, then shake with the rest and 1 cup of ice, or stir then add ice. Serve in a highball glass with a lime wedge.

Watermelon Cooler

2 slices of ripe Peach, muddled

¾ cup (6 oz) Watermelon Juice

1 Tbsp Lime Juice

2 counts Agave Syrup

Muddle 2 peach slices, then shake with the rest and 1 cup of ice, or stir then add ice. Serve in a highball glass with a lime wheel.

Herbal Teas

A great way to add traditional flavors to your beverages is to use herbal iced teas. Think of a cool Grasshopper (mint tea) and the perennial Harvey Wallbanger (licorice tea).

To make chilled tea for your Fresh Bar, steep a strong batch of hot tea, and then cool it in a refrigerator or by setting the whole container in a bin of ice. (Do not add ice to warm or hot tea, as this will dilute the flavor.) See Chapter 3 for Warm Drinks using herbal teas.

Harvey Wallbanger

½ cup (4 oz) Orange Juice

¼ cup (2 oz) strong Licorice Tea, chilled

1 count Agave Syrup

Shake with 1 cup of ice, or stir then add ice. Serve in a highball glass. Garnish with an orange wheel.

🍸 Fu Manchu

½ cup (4 oz) strong Mint Tea, chilled

¼ cup (2 oz) Orange Juice

4 Tbsp (1 ½ oz) Lime Juice

4 counts Agave Syrup

Stir and chill or shake with ice, and strain into a chilled martini glass. Garnish with a lime twist.

1 COUNT aGaVe SYRUP = a 1-SeconD SQUIRT see page 15

🥂 Banana-Rama

¾ cup (6 oz) strong Mint Tea, chilled

¼ cup (2 oz) Lime Juice

1 ripe Banana

4-6 frozen Peach slices

12 counts Agave Syrup

Blend with 1 ½ cups of ice and serve in a hurricane glass. Garnish with fresh mint and a lime wheel.

🥃 Cool Me Off

Fresh Mint

½ cup (4 oz) Orange Juice

¼ cup (2 oz) strong Mint Tea, chilled

2 counts Agave Syrup

Muddle several mint leaves, then shake the rest with 1 cup of ice, or stir then add ice. Serve in a highball glass with fresh mint and an orange wheel.

Swamp Water

1/3 cup (3 oz) Pineapple Juice

¼ cup (2 oz) strong Licorice Tea, chilled

2 Tbsp (¾ oz) Lime Juice

2 counts Agave Syrup

Dash of Allspice

Shake with 1 cup of ice, or stir then add ice. Serve in a highball glass with a lime wedge.

Brazilian Freeze

½ cup (4 oz) strong Licorice Tea, chilled

2 ripe Bananas

¼ cup (2 oz) Orange Juice

¼ cup (2 oz) Pineapple Juice

12 counts Agave Syrup

¼ inch Vanilla Bean (optional)

Blend with 1 ½ cups of ice and serve in a hurricane glass. Garnish with various fruits.

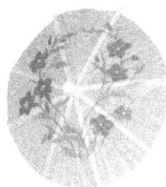

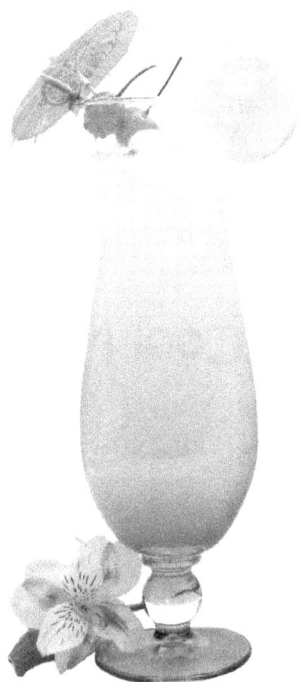

Flavored Agave Syrup

Expand your Fresh Bar offerings by creating flavored agave syrups ahead of time. Crème de Banana is common in tropical drinks, and coffee liqueurs are some of the most popular top-shelf cordials.

To make Banana Agave: Blend, or mash and whisk (if gooey), one medium overripe banana with ½ cup (4 oz) agave syrup. Store in a small squeeze bottle.

To make Espresso Agave: In a small mixing bowl, stir a double sized espresso with 1/3 cup agave syrup. Store in a small squeeze bottle.

In a squeeze bottle with a ¼-inch opening:

1 count Agave Syrup = A one-second squirt

12 counts flavored agave = ¼ cup

Island Splash

½ cup (4 oz) each Orange & Pineapple Juice

Splash (1 oz) Lemon Juice

6 counts Banana Agave

Shake with 2 cups of ice, or stir then add ice. Serve in a hurricane glass with a pineapple wedge or an orange wheel.

Good & Plenty

½ cup (4 oz) strong Licorice Tea, chilled

4 counts Espresso Agave

Shake or swirl with ice, and strain into a chilled cocktail glass.

⏚ Skittle

¼ cup (2 oz) Lemon Juice

4 Tbsp (1 ½ oz) Black Cherry Juice

2 counts Banana Agave

Shake or swirl with ice, and strain into a chilled cocktail glass.

Black Cherry Juice

Treat yourself and your Fresh Party guests to Black Cherry Rejuvenate by **Premier Research Labs**. This makes a wonderful (and tastier) substitute for traditional grenadine in your Fresh Bar. Simply cut a slit in the bottle's foil covering – this will help you to drizzle the brightly colored juice dramatically into your drinks.

PRL specializes in high quality, excipient-free, *cell-resonant* foods and whole food supplements. See the Resources section for some of my other favorite products from PRL, including Pomegranate Rejuvenate.

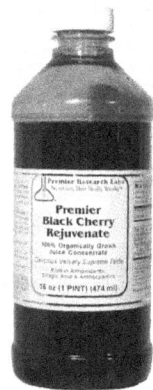

⏚ Fresh Hurricane

½ cup (4 oz) Orange Juice

½ cup (4 oz) Pineapple Juice

¼ cup (2 oz) Lime Juice

8 counts Agave Syrup

Black Cherry Juice to drizzle

Shake all except cherry juice with 2 cups of ice, or stir then add ice. Serve in a hurricane glass. Drizzle cherry juice over the top and garnish with a pineapple wedge or an orange wheel.

Y Cherry Melon

¾ cup (6 oz) Honeydew Melon Juice

Splash (1 oz) Orange Juice

Splash (1 oz) Black Cherry Juice

2 counts Agave Syrup

Stir and chill or shake with ice, then strain into a chilled martini glass. Garnish with a sword of cherries and melon pieces.

1 count agave syrup = a 1-second squirt see page 15

Y Sex on the Beach

½ cup (4 oz) Honeydew Melon Juice

¼ cup (2 oz) Orange Juice

Splash (1 oz) Lemon Juice

2 Tbsp (¾ oz) Black Cherry Juice

4 counts Agave Syrup

Stir and chill or shake with ice, then strain into a chilled martini glass. Garnish with a lemon twist.

Swinging Ape

A few slices of Banana, muddled

½ cup (4 oz) strong Mint Tea, chilled

2 Tbsp (¾ oz) of Black Cherry Juice

4 counts Banana Agave

Muddle a few slices of banana, then shake with the rest and 1 cup of ice, or stir then add ice. Serve in a highball glass with fresh mint.

Fourth of July

¾ cup (6 oz) strong Mint Tea, chilled

½ cup (4 oz) Orange Juice

4 counts Agave Syrup

Black Cherry Juice to drizzle

Shake all except cherry juice with 2 cups of ice and serve in a hurricane glass. Drizzle cherry juice over the top and garnish with an orange wheel.

Georgia Tea

Fresh Mint, muddled

½ cup (4 oz) strong Mint Tea, chilled

4 Tbsp (1 ½ oz) Lemon Juice

2 Tbsp (¾ oz) Black Cherry Juice

5 counts Agave Syrup

Muddle several mint leaves, then shake with the rest and 1 cup of ice, or stir then add ice. Serve in a highball glass with a lemon wedge.

Jelly Bean

¾ cup (6 oz) strong Licorice Tea, chilled

Splash (1 oz) Black Cherry Juice

3 counts Agave Syrup

Stir and chill or shake with ice, and strain into a chilled martini glass. Garnish with a lemon twist or a fresh cherry.

Chapter 2
Coconuts & Nut Creams

"No one ever found wisdom without also being a fool." - Erica Jong

Treat your Fresh Party guests to real coconut and nut creams, and you'll gain some loyal fans! Cream is a staple in traditional bars, and it's used in the most decadent drinks, from White Russians, Grasshoppers and Piña Coladas to Banana Banshees, Creamsicles and Spanish Coffees. In this chapter, I offer some tasty ideas for using fresh coconut *water* as well.

Cashew Cream is the easiest cream to make, so if you want to get your feet wet, you can start on page 40. I do recommend that you use a blender or a shaker to mix your juices with nut creams, as this will prevent separation; your other option is to add lecithin emulsifier to your nut creams when you make them (see page 50).

Obviously, coconuts can add a tropical flair to your Fresh Party. I highly recommend using the shell for serving drinks, either before or after removing the meat. If you leave the meat in, simply serve the beverage with a straw *and* a spoon.

⊔ Coco Mojito

Several fresh Mint Leaves

½ cup (4 oz) Coconut Water

4 Tbsp (1 ½ oz) Lime Juice

2 counts Agave Syrup

Muddle the mint, leaving the leaves mostly intact, then shake with the rest and 1 cup of ice, or stir then add ice. Serve in a highball glass with fresh mint leaves and a lime wedge.

Fresh Coconut

Fresh young coconuts will give a rich, tropical flavor to your Fresh Bar. These are also called "white" or "Thai" coconuts. They can generally be found in health food stores and Asian markets, or you can order a case on the internet and have it shipped to you.

Coconut water is simply the clear to slightly cloudy liquid inside every coconut, while *coconut cream* is created by blending the coconut meat with the water.

To open a young coconut, chop with a cleaver or large knife around the coconut's pointed tip until you can pry off a round chunk of the shell and husk. The quickest way I've found is to use the 90-degree cleaver edge nearest the handle to penetrate the husk all around the tip.

I always use young coconuts (as opposed to the mature brown ones) because the meat is sweeter, softer and easier to blend. Here's how I use a case of coconuts (usually nine in number):

- Open the coconuts and save the water for drinks
- Blend the softest meat from 2 coconuts with about 2 cups of the water for each batch of cream
- Use the hard meat chunks, if any, for garnishes and munchies

To make Coconut Cream, blend one coconut's water (about 2 cups) with the meat of two coconuts. If you're using a standard kitchen blender, choose about 2 coconuts worth of the softest meat among them. For individual blended drinks, you can simply blend the water (or juice) and meat as you create each beverage, as noted in the recipes.

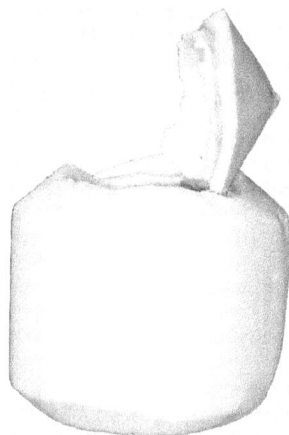

♟ Dance the Night Away

½ cup (4 oz) Coconut Water

3 counts Espresso Agave

Shake or swirl over ice, and strain into a chilled cocktail glass.

♟ Strawberry Colada

1 ¼ cup Pineapple Juice

Meat from 1 young Coconut

2/3 cup Strawberries, frozen

8 counts Agave Syrup

Blend juice and coconut first, then blend in strawberries and 1 cup of ice. Serve in a hurricane glass. Garnish with a whole strawberry or a pineapple wedge.

♟ Mai Tai

½ cup (4 oz) Coconut Water

½ cup (4 oz) Orange Juice

Splash (1 oz) Lime Juice

2 counts Agave Syrup

Black Cherry Juice to drizzle

Shake all except cherry juice with 2 cups of ice, or stir then add ice. Serve in a hurricane glass. Drizzle cherry juice over the top and garnis with an orange wheel.

♼ Coco Kamikaze

½ cup (4 oz) Coconut Water

¼ cup (2 oz) Orange Juice

¼ cup (2 oz) Lime Juice

3 counts Agave Syrup

Stir and chill or shake with ice, and strain into a chilled martini glass. Garnish with a lime twist.

1 COUNT
AGAVE SYRUP
= A 1-SECOND
SQUIRT
see page 15

♼ Coco-Berry Freeze

Meat from 1 young Coconut

1 cup Orange Juice

4 Tbsp (1 ½ oz) Lemon Juice

10 counts Agave Syrup

2/3 cup frozen Blueberries or Mixed Berries

Blend juices and coconut first, then blend in berries and 1 cup of ice. Serve in a hurricane glass. Garnish with an orange wheel.

♼ Pina Colada Straight Up

¾ cup (6 oz) Pineapple Juice

¼ cup (2 oz) Coconut Cream

2 counts Agave Syrup

Stir and chill or shake with ice, and strain into a martini glass. Garnish with a small pineapple wedge.

⟁ Flying Kangaroo

½ cup (4 oz) Pineapple Juice

¼ cup (2 oz) strong Licorice Tea, chilled

¼ cup (2 oz) Coconut Cream

1 count Agave Syrup

Stir and chill or shake with ice, and strain into a chilled martini glass. Garnish with a lime wedge.

♟ Apple Colada

½ cup (4 oz) Apple Juice

½ cup (4 oz) Coconut Cream

¼ cup (2 oz) Pineapple Juice

2 counts Agave Syrup, only if using tart apples

Shake with 2 cups of ice, or stir then add ice. Serve in a hurricane glass. Garnish with a pineapple wedge and a fresh pitted cherry.

♟ Bahama Mama

½ cup (4 oz) Orange Juice

½ cup (4 oz) Pineapple Juice

¼ cup (2 oz) Coconut Cream

2 counts Agave Syrup

Black Cherry Juice to drizzle

Shake all except cherry juice with 2 cups of ice, or stir then add ice. Serve in a hurricane glass. Drizzle cherry juice over the top and garnish with a pineapple wedge.

⏲ Banana Java

1 cup Coconut Water + the meat of ½ young Coconut

8 counts Espresso Agave

2 Bananas

Blend without ice first, then blend in 1 ½ cups of ice and serve in a hurricane glass. Garnish with an orange wheel.

⏲ Southern Breeze

1 cup Pineapple Juice

Splash (1 oz) Black Cherry Juice

Meat of ½ young Coconut

1 ripe Banana

8 counts Agave Syrup

½ cup frozen Peach slices

1 COUNT aGave SYRUP = a 1-SeCOND SQUIRT
see page 15

Blend without ice and peaches first, then blend with 1 cup ice and serve in a hurricane glass. Garnish with an orange wheel.

⏲ Strawberries ♦ Cream

¾ cup (6 oz) Coconut Water + the meat of ½ young Coconut

4 Tbsp (1 ½ oz) each Black Cherry Juice and Lemon Juice

8 counts Agave Syrup

6 large Strawberries, fresh or frozen

Blend liquids with coconut meat first, then add berries and 2 cups of ice. Serve in a hurricane glass. Garnish with a fresh strawberry.

🥛 Flying Monkey

Several Banana slices, muddled

1/3 cup (3 oz) Orange Juice

1/3 cup (3 oz) Coconut Water

3 counts Banana Agave

Muddle the banana, then shake with the rest and 1 cup of ice, or stir then add ice. Serve in a highball glass with an orange slice.

Jamaican Rum Spice

This exotic spice blend will give a Caribbean flair to your Fresh Bar offerings, without any actual rum!

Jamaican Rum Spice can be purchased at spicebarn.com. Alternatively, you can use allspice and a couple drops of vanilla extract. While you're online, pick up an empty bottle with a glass dropper, to help with measuring, at mountainroseherbs.com.

For multiplying recipes: **50 drops = ¼ tsp**

🥂 Hot Jamaican

½ cup (4 oz) each Coconut Water & Pineapple Juice

¼ cup (2 oz) Lime Juice

1 tsp Ginger Juice

4 counts Agave Syrup

25 drops (1/8 tsp) Jamaican Rum Spice or a dash of Allspice

Shake with 2 cups of ice, or stir then add ice. Serve in a hurricane glass. Garnish with a pineapple wedge or a lime wheel.

Pirate's Holiday

1 COUNT
AGAVE SYRUP
= a 1-second
SQUIRT
see page 15

Several Banana slices, muddled

½ cup (4 oz) Coconut Water

Splash (1 oz) Lime Juice

4 counts Banana Agave

12 drops Jamaican Rum Spice, or Vanilla Extract and Allspice

Muddle the banana, then shake with the rest and 1 cup of ice, or stir then add ice. Serve in a highball glass with a lime wedge.

Caribbean Dream

½ cup (4 oz) Coconut Cream

2 counts Banana Agave

12 drops Jamaican Rum Spice or a dash of Allspice

Stir and chill or shake with ice, and strain into chilled cocktail glass. Garnish with a sprinkle of allspice over the top.

Pacific Cruise

½ cup (4 oz) Orange Juice

½ cup (4 oz) Pineapple Juice

Meat from ½ young coconut

½ cup frozen Pineapple chunks

25 drops (1/8 tsp) Jamaican Rum Spice or a dash of Allspice

10 counts Agave Syrup

Blend without ice first, then blend in 1 ½ cups of ice and serve in a hurricane glass. Garnish with a pineapple wedge.

Zombie

½ cup (4 oz) Pineapple Juice

¼ cup (2 oz) Orange Juice

¼ cup (2 oz) Coconut Cream

Splash (1 oz) Lime Juice

4 counts Agave Syrup

25 drops (1/8 tsp) Jamaican Rum Spice or a dash of Allspice

Shake with 2 cups of ice, or stir then add ice. Serve in a hurricane glass. Garnish with an orange wheel.

Cacao Powder

Cacao powder from unprocessed, unroasted beans is a luxury for the taste buds, and it's super-high in antioxidants and magnesium. Get the highest quality raw cacao powder from Sunfood Nutrition (see Resources).

If you use regular, roasted cacao powder, the taste will be stronger, so reduce the amount in the recipe by about half. Either way, ***shake vigorously!***

Good Morning Lift

1 cup Coconut Water

6 counts Banana Agave

½ Tbsp raw Cacao Powder

25 drops (1/8 tsp) Jamaican Rum Spice or a dash of Allspice

Shake vigorously with ice, and strain into a chilled martini glass.

🥛 Banana Boat

¼ cup (2 oz) strong Mint Tea, chilled

4 Tbsp (1 ½ oz) Coconut Cream

3 counts Banana Agave

Splash (1 oz) Orange Juice

12 drops Jamaican Rum Spice or a dash of Allspice

Shake with 1 cup of ice, or stir then add ice. Serve in a highball glass. Garnish with an orange slice.

🍷 Bob Marley

½ cup (4 oz) strong Mint Tea, chilled

¾ cup (6 oz) Coconut Cream

4 counts Agave Syrup

25 drops (1/8 tsp) Jamaican Rum Spice or a dash of Allspice

Shake with 2 cups of ice, or stir then add ice. Serve in a hurricane glass with an orange wheel and a sprinkle of raw cacao powder.

🍸 Spiced Coconut Cooler

¾ cup (6 oz) Coconut Water

½ cup (4 oz) Pineapple Juice

25 drops (1/8 tsp) Jamaican Rum Spice or a dash of Allspice

2 counts Agave Syrup

Black Cherry Juice to drizzle

Shake all but cherry juice with 2 cups ice, or stir then add ice. Serve in a hurricane glass with pineapple and a drizzle of cherry juice.

Nut Creams

Homemade nut creams will add rich and distinctive flavors to your Fresh Bar. To make a high-enzyme fresh cream, soak raw nuts for 8-12 hours before blending.

Raw cashews are among the richer nuts, so they'll break down easily and completely in your blender. They have a mild, "invisible" flavor and are relatively easy to find. They'll make a rich, general purpose cream for your Fresh Bar.

To make Cashew Cream: Simply blend 1 cup of soaked cashews with 1 ½ cups fresh water and 2 second-counts of agave syrup until smooth, and then chill.

Almonds and hazelnuts will not break down completely in even the highest horsepower blenders. A fine kitchen strainer will remove the largest nut pieces left after blending, but the only way to create a really smooth cream from these hard nuts will be to use a Nut Milk Bag. Raw almonds are often favored because they're alkalizing.

A Nut Milk/Sprout Bag is a very fine nylon mesh bag used for straining nut milks and sprouting grains and seeds. (Burlap sprouting bags won't work for straining nut creams.) See the Resources section for sources.

To make Almond or Hazelnut Cream: Blend 1 cup of soaked nuts really well with 1 ½ cups of water (or coconut water) and 2 second-counts of agave syrup. Strain through a nylon mesh bag. You can add a few drops of almond or hazelnut extract, if desired. To make it thicker, blend with 1/3 cup soaked cashews. *Note:* Leftover nut pulp can be used in Fresh Party Bites (see Chapter 7).

Flavored Nut Creams are great for some blended and warm drinks. Simply blend nuts with juice instead of water, or add spices. See Chapter 3 for Warm Drink recipes.

Frozen Banana Banshee

1 COUNT
agave SYRUP
= a 1-second
SQUIRT
see page 15

¾ cup (6 oz) Nut Cream

2 ripe Bananas

1 Tbsp raw Cacao Powder

2 counts Agave Syrup

Blend with 1 ½ cups of ice until smooth and serve in a hurricane glass. Garnish with an orange wheel.

Banana Banshee Cocktail

¾ cup (6 oz) Nut Cream

8 counts Banana Agave

2 tsp raw Cacao Powder

Shake vigorously with ice, and strain into a chilled martini glass. Garnish with a banana wheel (a thick slice of banana with the peel).

Blackberry Freeze

1 cup Orange Juice

½ cup Cashews, soaked 8-12 hours and rinsed

½ cup frozen Blackberries or Mixed Berries

8 counts Agave Syrup

Dash of Nutmeg

Blend orange juice and cashews first, then blend in the rest with 1 ½ cups of ice and serve in a hurricane glass. Garnish with an orange wheel.

Creamsicle

¾ cup (6 oz) Orange Juice

½ cup (4 oz) strong Licorice Tea, chilled

½ cup Cashews, soaked 8-12 hours and rinsed

½ inch Vanilla Bean

8 counts Agave Syrup

Blend ingredients without ice, then blend in 1 ½ cups of ice. Serve in a hurricane glass. Garnish with an orange wheel.

Golden Cadillac

½ cup (4 oz) strong Licorice Tea, chilled

½ cup (4 oz) Nut Cream

2 tsp raw Cacao Powder

6 counts Agave Syrup

Shake vigorously with ice, and strain into a chilled martini glass. Garnish with a sprinkle of cacao powder and an orange slice.

Bee Stinger

½ cup (4 oz) strong Mint Tea, chilled

4 Tbsp (1 ½ oz) Nut Cream

2 Tbsp (¾ oz) Black Cherry Juice

1 count Agave Syrup

Shake with 1 cup of ice, or stir then add ice. Serve in a highball glass. Garnish with a fresh pitted cherry.

♉ Crème de la Crème

**1 COUNT
aGave SYRUP
= a 1-second
SQUIRT**
see page 15

½ cup (4 oz) Orange Juice

½ cup (4 oz) Pineapple Juice

½ cup Cashews, soaked 8-12 hours and rinsed

1 cup frozen Strawberries

8 counts Agave Syrup

Blend juices with cashews first, then blend the rest with 1 cup of ice and serve in a hurricane glass. Garnish with a fresh strawberry.

♉ Bouncing Cherry

1/3 cup (3 oz) Nut Cream

2 Tbsp (¾ oz) Black Cherry Juice

2 counts Espresso Agave

Shake or swirl with ice and strain into a chilled cocktail glass.

♉ Aztec Gold

¼ cup (2 oz) Nut Cream

¼ cup (2 oz) Orange Juice

2 counts Espresso Agave

1 tsp raw Cacao Powder

Shake vigorously with ice and strain into a chilled cocktail glass. Garnish with a sprinkle of cacao powder.

🍸 Frozen Grasshopper

1 cup strong Mint Tea, chilled

½ cup Cashews, soaked 8-12 hours and rinsed

2 tsp raw Cacao Powder

2 counts Agave Syrup

Blend the tea and cashews first, then blend in the rest with 2 cups of ice. Serve in a hurricane glass. Garnish with fresh mint leaves.

🍸 Grasshopper Cocktail

¾ cup (6 oz) strong Mint Tea, chilled

¼ cup (2 oz) Nut Cream

2 counts Espresso Agave,

OR 1 tsp Raw Cacao Powder + 1 count Agave Syrup

If using espresso agave, simply shake or swirl ingredients with ice and strain into a chilled martini glass. If using cacao powder, shake vigorously and strain into a chilled martini glass. Garnish with fresh mint and a sprinkle of cacao powder.

Seabreeze ala Mode

1 COUNT
aGave SYRUP
= a 1-second
SQUIRT
see page 15

1/3 cup (3 oz) Pineapple Juice

1/3 cup (3 oz) Nut Cream

2 Tbsp (¾ oz) pure Cranberry Juice

3 counts Agave Syrup

Shake with 1 cup of ice, or stir then add ice. Serve in a highball glass with a pineapple wedge.

Cherry Blossom

½ cup (4 oz) Nut Cream

1/3 cup (3 oz) Orange Juice

Splash (1 oz) Cherry Juice

1 count Agave Syrup

Stir and chill or shake with ice, and strain into a chilled martini glass. Garnish with an orange slice.

Heavenly Spirits

½ cup (4 oz) Orange Juice

¼ cup (2 oz) Nut Cream

¼ cup (2 oz) Licorice Tea

1 Tbsp Black Cherry Juice (optional)

2 counts Agave Syrup

Stir and chill or shake with ice, and strain into a chilled martini glass. Garnish with an orange slice and a sprinkle of nutmeg.

Bit-O-Honey

3 oz sweet Apple Juice

1 oz Nut Cream

1 count Agave Syrup or 1 tsp Honey

Cinnamon to garnish

Stir and chill or shake with ice, and strain into a chilled cocktail glass. Garnish with a sprinkle of cinnamon.

Black Forest Cocktail

¾ cup (6 oz) Nut Cream

Splash (1 oz) Black Cherry Juice

2 Tbsp (¾ oz) Lemon Juice

½ Tbsp raw Cacao Powder

4 counts Agave Syrup

Shake vigorously with ice and strain into a chilled martini glass. Garnish with a sprinkle of cacao powder.

Bungee Jump

¾ cup (6 oz) Orange Juice

½ cup (4 oz) Nut Cream

2 counts Agave Syrup

Dash of Nutmeg

Shake with 2 cups of ice, or stir then add ice. Serve in a hurricane glass and garnish with an orange wheel.

Chapter 3
Warm Drinks

"Take care of the luxuries, and the necessities will take care of themselves." - Dorothy Parker

Warm beverages are wonderful for cold weather or breezy nights, or even for weekend brunch events. Common alcoholic additions to coffee include Kahlua, Bailey's, Triple Sec, brandy and Irish whiskey, among others.

As you can tell from the recipes on the following page, you can make one batch of flavored creamer to create several different beverages. Simply serve sweeteners and other additives on the side and give your guests their choice of hot tea or coffee.

I've also included a recommendation for a lecithin emulsifier on page 50, as well as a mulled wine recipe on page 54.

Café di Amaretto

Hot Coffee

Almond Cream* with Almond Extract and Cinnamon

Make almond cream with a few drops of almond extract and 1 Tbsp of cinnamon. Serve as a creamer for coffee with extra sweetener on the side.

* For complete instructions on how to make nut creams, see page 40.

Peppermint Patty

Peppermint Tea

Nut Cream* with raw Cacao Powder

Make a batch of nut cream with 2 Tbsp cacao powder. Serve as a creamer for tea with sweetener on the side.

Belgian Coffee

Hot Peppermint Tea

Nut Cream* with raw Cacao Powder

Espresso Agave

Make a batch of nut cream with 2 Tbsp cacao powder. Serve as a creamer for tea with Espresso Agave on the side.

Jaguar

Hot Licorice Tea

Nut Cream* with raw Cacao Powder

Make a batch of nut cream with 2 Tbsp cacao powder. Serve as a creamer for tea with sweetener on the side.

Beach Warmer

Hot Coffee

Nut Cream* with raw Cacao Powder

Black Cherry Juice

Blend a batch of nut cream with 2 Tbsp cacao powder. Serve as a creamer for coffee with cherry juice on the side.

🍶Speedboat

Hot Licorice Tea

Coconut Cream^

Espresso Agave

Serve Coconut Cream as a creamer for tea with Espresso Agave on the side.

🍶Jamaican Nights

Hot Licorice Tea

Pineapple Coconut Cream^ with Rum Spice or Allspice

Make coconut cream with pineapple juice as a base, instead of coconut water, and add 1 tsp of Jamaican Rum Spice, or 1 tsp of Allspice plus a few drops of vanilla extract. Serve as a creamer for tea with sweetener on the side.

Lecithin Emulsifier

An emulsifier is a substance or process that helps water and oil to mix, such as watery teas and coffees with rich creamers. Commercial creamers are either homogenized or have added emulsifiers. Honey is a natural emulsifier, and the act of vigorously shaking a drink can have the same effect.

Liquid lecithin is an additive that will help your fresh creamers blend well with hot teas and coffee, and any other non-shaken beverage or juice. This lecithin is the consistency of honey, so just add a tiny dab to a batch of nut or coconut cream. As a result, your guests will see no unsightly separation (which can look like curdling).

Coffee

The popularity of coffee is at an all-time high in America, so some of your Fresh Party guests may consider it a treat. Though coffee contains harsh acids and oils, on the plus side, its antioxidant levels are (like those of cacao) simply off the charts. You can choose coffee that's organically grown, not over-roasted, and of a low-acid variety. Try Premier Coffee by Premier Research Labs (see Resources section) or one that's freshly roasted in your local area.

Caribbean Night

Hot Coffee

Coconut Cream^ with Raw Cacao Powder

Banana Agave

Blend a batch of Coconut Cream with 2 Tablespoons of cacao powder. Serve the cream and Banana Agave on the side.

Caribbean Coffee

Hot Coffee

Orange Coconut Cream^ with Rum Spice or Allspice

Make coconut cream with orange juice as a base, instead of coconut water, and add 1 tsp Jamaican Rum Spice or 1 tsp Allspice. Serve as a creamer for coffee with sweetener on the side.

^ *For complete instructions on how to make coconut cream, see page 31.*

Dinner Mint

Hot Mint Tea

Orange Nut Cream*

Espresso Agave

Make nut cream with orange juice as a base, instead of water. Serve as a creamer for tea with Espresso Agave on the side.

Spanish Coffee

Hot Coffee

Orange Nut Cream*

Nutmeg

Espresso Agave (optional)

Make nut cream with orange juice as a base, instead of water. Serve as a creamer for coffee with sweetener and nutmeg on the side. Or, blend 2 tsp of nutmeg into the nut cream.

Boston Tea

Hot Black Tea

Orange Nut Cream*

Ground Cloves

Make nut cream with orange juice as a base, instead of water. Serve as a creamer for tea with sweetener and ground cloves on the side. Or, blend 2 tsp of ground cloves into the nut cream.

* For complete instructions on how to make nut creams, see page 40.

Vanilla Mocha

Hot Coffee

Nut Cream* with Vanilla Bean and raw Cacao Powder

Make nut cream with ½ inch vanilla bean and 2 Tbsp raw cacao powder. Serve as a creamer with extra sweetener on the side.

Nutty Spiced Coffee

Hot Coffee

Nut Cream* with Vanilla Bean and Spices

Almond or Hazelnut Extract (optional)

Make nut cream with ½ inch vanilla bean and 1 tsp each cinnamon and cardamom. Add a few drops of almond or hazelnut extract, if desired. Serve as a creamer with extra sweetener on the side.

Tahoe Nights

Hot Coffee

Nut Cream* with Maple and Cherry

Make a batch of nut cream with only 1 cup water, ¼ cup maple syrup and ¼ cup Black Cherry Juice (no agave syrup). Serve as a creamer for coffee.

🍺Anna's Mulled Wine

3 bottles of Burgundy or Cabernet Sauvignon Red Wine

2 organic Oranges, cut in 8 wedges each

5 large Cinnamon Sticks

25 whole Cloves (with the tops still on)

3 cups organic white or brown Sugar

Optional: Lemon Rind, whole Allspice, Juniper Berries, Nutmeg

Combine ingredients in a non-aluminum pan and bring to a boil. Cover, reduce heat and simmer for 20 minutes, stirring frequently. Remove from heat and allow to cool, covered, until it reaches drinking temperature. Strain out cinnamon sticks and cloves, and squeeze the juice from the orange wedges into the wine. Serve warm.

54   **THE FRESH BARTENDER**

Chapter 4
Kombucha Coolers

"If you always do what interests you, at least one person is pleased." - Katharine Hepburn

It's fun to make drinks with fermented, enzyme-rich kombucha because the fermentation gives a tangy "bite" reminiscent of alcoholic beverages. You can purchase a case of bottled kombucha to serve at your Fresh Party, or you can make your own (see Appendix I).

Kombucha is the Western name for sweetened tea that has been fermented using a large solid mass of microorganisms called a "kombucha colony." The culture itself looks somewhat like a large pancake, and though often called a mushroom, it is simply a fungus.

Kombucha may contain some of the following components depending on the source of the culture: Acetic acid, which provides anti-microbial activity; B-vitamins; beneficial probiotics; live active enzymes; L-Theanine (an amino acid); and polyphenols.

The recorded history of this drink dates back to the Qin Dynasty in China (around 250 BC). The Chinese called kombucha the "Immortal Health Elixir," because they believed it balanced the Middle Qi (spleen and stomach) and aided in digestion, allowing the body to focus on healing.

ᛉ Cosmopolitan

Splash (1 oz) pure Cranberry Juice

Splash (1 oz) Lemon Juice

8 counts Agave Syrup

¾ cup (6 oz) Kombucha

Shake or stir the juices and agave with ice, then add kombucha and strain into a chilled martini glass. Garnish with a lemon twist.

Frozen Margarita

½ cup (4 oz) Kombucha

¼ cup (2 oz) Orange Juice

¼ cup (2 oz) Lemon Juice

¼ cup (2 oz) Lime Juice

10 counts Agave Syrup

Blend with 2 cups of ice and serve in a hurricane glass. Garnish with a lime wheel.

1 COUNT AGAVE SYRUP = a 1-SECOND SQUIRT
see page 15

Tsunami

¼ cup (2 oz) Pineapple Juice

4 Tbsp (1 ½ oz) Orange Juice

4 counts Agave Syrup

½ cup (4 oz) Kombucha

Shake or stir the juices and agave with ice, then add kombucha and strain into a chilled martini glass. Garnish with an orange slice.

Beach Bar Special

½ cup (4 oz) Orange Juice

1/3 cup (3 oz) Coconut Water

25 drops (1/8 tsp) Jamaican Rum Spice or a dash of Allspice

3 counts Agave Syrup

1/3 cup (3 oz) Kombucha

Shake the juices, agave and spice with 2 cups of ice, then add kombucha and serve in a hurricane glass. Garnish with an orange wheel.

🥃 Seaside Cooler

Fresh Mint

¼ cup (2 oz) strong Mint Tea, chilled

4 Tbsp (1 ½ oz) Orange Juice

3 counts Agave Syrup

¼ cup (2 oz) Kombucha

Muddle a few mint leaves, then shake with all but kombucha and 1 cup of ice, or stir then add ice. Pour into a highball glass with kombucha. Garnish with fresh mint and an orange slice.

🍹 Pineapple Margarita

½ cup (4 oz) Pineapple Juice

4 Tbsp (1 ½ oz) Lime Juice

6 counts Agave Syrup

½ cup (4 oz) Kombucha

Shake juices and agave with 2 cups of ice, or stir then add ice.
Add kombucha and serve in a hurricane glass. Garnish with a pineapple wedge.

Kombucha Berry Freeze

1 cup Kombucha

¼ cup (2 oz) Lemon Juice

1 cup frozen Strawberries or Mixed Berries

8 counts Agave Syrup

Blend with 1 cup of ice and serve in a hurricane glass. Garnish with a whole strawberry.

Honeydew Cooler

½ cup (4 oz) Honeydew Melon Juice

Splash (1 oz) Lemon Juice

Splash (1 oz) Orange Juice

3 counts Agave Syrup

½ cup (4 oz) Kombucha

1 COUNT
aGave SYRUP
= a 1-second
SQUIRT
see page 15

Shake juices and agave with 2 cups of ice, or stir then add ice. Add kombucha and serve in a hurricane glass with an orange wheel.

Banana Bomb

A few slices of Banana

½ cup (4 oz) strong Mint Tea, chilled

4 counts Banana Agave

¼ cup (2 oz) Kombucha

Muddle banana, then shake with the tea and agave and 1 cup of ice, or stir then add ice. Add kombucha and serve in a highball glass. Garnish with a lime wedge.

🍸 Raspberry Margarita

¾ cup (6 oz) Kombucha

¼ cup (2 oz) Orange Juice

4 Tbsp (1 ½ oz) Lime Juice

1 cup frozen Raspberries

10 counts Agave Syrup

Blend with 1 cup of ice and serve in a hurricane glass. Garnish with a lime wheel.

🍸 Frozen Matador

¾ cup (6 oz) Kombucha

¼ cup (2 oz) Pineapple Juice

¼ cup (2 oz) Lime Juice

½ cup frozen Black Cherries or Raspberries

½ cup frozen Pineapple

10 counts Agave Syrup

Blend with 1 cup of ice and serve in a hurricane glass. Garnish with a pineapple wedge.

🍸 Kamikaze

¼ cup (2 oz) Orange Juice

4 Tbsp (1 ½ oz) Lime Juice

4 counts Agave Syrup

½ cup (4 oz) Kombucha

Shake juices and agave with ice, or stir then add ice to chill. Add kombucha and strain into a chilled martini glass. Garnish with a lime wheel.

Gingerberry Freeze

1 COUNT AGAVE SYRUP = A 1-SECOND SQUIRT
see page 15

1 cup Kombucha

4 Tbsp (1 ½ oz) Lemon Juice

1 Tbsp grated Ginger

2/3 cup frozen Raspberries or Mixed Berries

12 counts Agave Syrup

Blend with 1 ½ cups of ice and serve in a hurricane glass. Garnish with a spear of whole raspberries.

Gingersnap

4 Tbsp (1 ½ oz) Pineapple Juice

2 Tbsp (¾ oz) Lemon Juice

1 tsp fresh Ginger Juice

4 counts Agave Syrup

¼ cup (2 oz) Kombucha

Shake juices and agave with ice, then add kombucha and strain into a chilled cocktail glass. Garnish with a lemon twist.

🥃 Lynchburg Kombucha

¼ cup (2 oz) Lemon Juice

Splash (1 oz) Orange Juice

4 counts Agave Syrup

1/3 cup (3 oz) Kombucha

Shake juices and agave with 1 cup of ice, or stir then add ice. Add kombucha and serve in a highball glass with a lemon wedge.

🥂 Georgia Margarita

¾ cup (6 oz) Kombucha

¼ cup (2 oz) Lemon Juice

¼ cup (2 oz) Orange Juice

1 cup sliced Peaches, frozen

10 counts Agave Syrup

Blend with 1 cup of ice and serve in a hurricane glass. Garnish with a lime wheel.

🥂 Pink Lemonade

¼ cup (2 oz) Lemon Juice

Splash (1 oz) pure Cranberry Juice

6 counts Agave Syrup

¾ cup (6 oz) Kombucha

Shake juices and agave with a little ice, or stir then add ice. Add kombucha and up to 2 cups of ice total, and serve in a hurricane glass. Garnish with a lemon wedge.

☼ Ladies Cocktail

1 COUNT
aGave SYRUP
= a 1-second
SQUIRT
see page 15

¼ cup (2 oz) strong Licorice Tea, chilled

¼ cup (2 oz) Pineapple Juice

2 counts Agave Syrup

½ cup (4 oz) Kombucha

Shake or stir juices, tea and agave with ice, then add kombucha and strain into a chilled martini glass. Garnish with a lemon twist.

☼ Kombucha Sunrise

½ cup (4 oz) Orange Juice

3 counts Agave Syrup

¼ cup (2 oz) Kombucha

Black Cherry Juice to drizzle

Shake orange juice and agave with 1 cup of ice, or stir then add ice. Add kombucha and pour into a highball glass. Drizzle cherry juice over the top and garnish with an orange wheel.

☼ Kombucha Cooler

¼ cup (2 oz) Pineapple Juice

2 Tbsp (¾ oz) Lemon Juice

1 Tbsp Black Cherry Juice

4 counts Agave Syrup

1/3 cup (3 oz) Kombucha

Shake juices and agave with 1 cup of ice, or stir then add ice. Add kombucha and serve in a highball glass with a pineapple wedge.

♟ Singapore Sling

2 Tbsp (¾ oz) Lemon Juice

2 Tbsp (¾ oz) Lime Juice

2 Tbsp (¾ oz) Black Cherry Juice

6 counts Agave Syrup

1 cup Kombucha

Shake or stir juices and agave with a little ice, then add kombucha and ice to 2 cups total. Serve in a hurricane glass with a lime wheel.

♟ Cherry Martini

Splash (1 oz) Black Cherry Juice

2 Tbsp (¾ oz) Lime Juice

4 counts Agave Syrup

¾ cup (6 oz) Kombucha

Shake or stir juices and agave with ice, then add kombucha and strain into a chilled martini glass. Garnish with a twist of lime.

♟ Red Hat Cocktail

1/3 cup (3 oz) Pink Grapefruit Juice

2 Tbsp (¾ oz) Cherry Juice

3 counts Agave Syrup

½ cup (4 oz) Kombucha

Shake juices and agave with ice, or stir then add ice. Add kombucha and strain into a chilled martini glass. Garnish with a thick grapefruit slice, a fresh pitted cherry and a parasol.

Chapter 5
Wine Drinks

"Quickly, bring me
a beaker of wine,
so that I may wet
my mind and say
something clever."
- Aristophanes

Wine is indeed a raw (uncooked), fermented beverage, with ancient roots in many human cultures. Archaeological evidence suggests that the earliest wine production came from sites in Iran and Georgia dating from 6000 to 5000 BC.

Research studies indicate that drinking red wine moderately (two to three glasses per day) can help lower cholesterol, decrease the risk of coronary heart disease and help us live longer. The same antioxidants found in regular wine also exist in alcohol-free wine, including resveratrol (a constituent of red wine), which in mouse and rat experiments, manifests anti-cancer, anti-inflammatory, blood-sugar-lowering and other beneficial cardiovascular effects. Those who are allergic to sulfites will also find an added health benefit in wines designated "organic."

To produce wine, harvested grapes are crushed and allowed to ferment while yeast converts most of the sugars in the grape juice into alcohol. After the primary fermentation, the liquid is transferred to vessels for the secondary fermentation. The accumulation of alcohol will kill the yeast when it reaches a concentration between 14-18%, stopping the fermentation. Champagne is a sparkling wine produced by inducing secondary fermentation of wine in the bottle to effect carbonation.

An alcohol-free wine beverage is produced by diluting a table wine with demineralized water and feeding the diluted wine to a centrifugal film evaporator where alcohol is stripped from the wine. The wine base is then mixed with concentrated grape juice.

When buying a quality wine, the label should give you information as to how dry it is (dry is the opposite of sweet) and which flavors characterize the wine. For instance, a bottle of wine I recently purchased says that it "displays the classic flavors of kiwi, pineapple and peaches," which sounds like a dessert or party punch wine to me!

▼ Mimosa

Fresh Orange Juice

Organic White Wine or Champagne

Fill a chilled wine glass with ¼ orange juice and the rest with wine. If using champagne, do not add ice. Garnish with an orange slice.

▼ Kir Royale

2 Tbsp (¾ oz) Black Cherry Juice

1 count Agave Syrup

Organic White Wine or Champagne

1 count agave syrup = a 1-second squirt
see page 15

If using wine, shake or stir ingredients lightly with a few ice cubes and serve in a large chilled wine glass. If serving champagne, drizzle the cherry juice and agave syrup slowly into the champagne; you can give it a light stirring with a spoon if needed, but don't shake it or add ice. Garnish with a lemon twist.

▼ Poinsettia

½ cup (4 oz) White Wine

1/3 cup (3 oz) Orange Juice

Splash (1 oz) pure Cranberry Juice

3 counts Agave Syrup

Shake or stir lightly with ice and strain into a chilled martini glass. Garnish with a lemon twist.

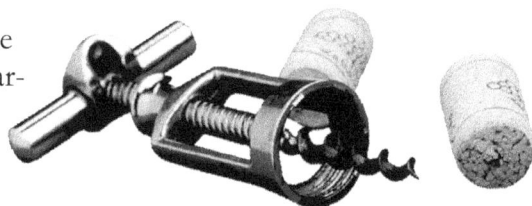

Wine Cooler

¾ cup (6 oz) White Wine

¼ cup (2 oz) Apple Juice

Splash (1 oz) Orange Juice

1 Tbsp Lemon Juice

2 counts Agave Syrup

Shake or stir lightly with ice. Strain into a large wine glass, adding several of the ice cubes to the beverage. Garnish with a lemon slice.

Wine Cooler II

¾ cup (6 oz) Sweet Wine, like a Riesling

¼ cup (2 oz) Pineapple Juice

Splash (1 oz) Lime or Lemon Juice

1 count Agave Syrup

Shake or stir lightly with ice. Strain into a large wine glass, adding several of the ice cubes to the beverage. Garnish with a lime slice.

Strawberry Slush

2 Strawberries, fresh or thawed frozen

1 Tbsp Black Cherry Juice

2 counts Agave Syrup

White Wine

Muddle a few strawberries in your shaker with the cherry juice and agave. Add wine and a little ice, shake or stir lightly and serve in a large wine glass. Garnish with a whole strawberry.

Frozen Peach

1 COUNT
AGAVE SYRUP
= a 1-SECOND
SQUIRT
see page 15

1 cup White Wine

¼ cup (2 oz) Orange Juice

1 cup frozen Peach slices

3 counts Agave syrup

Blend with 1 cup of ice and serve in a hurricane glass. Garnish with a lime wheel.

Caribbean Cocktail

½ cup (4 oz) White Wine

¼ cup (2 oz) Coconut Cream

¼ cup (2 oz) Orange Juice

6 counts Banana Agave

Shake or stir lightly with ice and strain into a chilled martini glass. Garnish with a dusting of allspice and an orange slice.

Miami Buzz

½ cup (4 oz) White Wine

1/3 cup (3 oz) Coconut Cream

4 Tbsp (1 ½ oz) Orange Juice

4 Tbsp (1 ½ oz) Grapefruit Juice

4 counts Agave Syrup

Shake lightly with 2 cups of ice, or stir then add ice. Serve in a hurricane glass. Garnish with a grapefruit or orange slice.

Cream of Cherry

½ cup (4 oz) White Wine

¼ cup (2 oz) Nut Cream

Splash (1 oz) Black Cherry Juice

2 counts Agave Syrup

Shake or stir lightly with ice and strain into a chilled martini glass. Garnish with a fresh pitted cherry.

Peppermint Fresh

Fresh Mint

1 Tbsp Lemon Juice (or 2 tsp in a small flute glass)

2 counts Agave Syrup

Champagne

Muddle a few mint leaves in your shaker, then swirl with lemon juice and agave syrup. Add to a chilled wine glass or flute and add champagne. Garnish with fresh mint.

Sangria Blanca

2 bottles White Wine

1 Tbsp Lemon Juice

1 cup thinly sliced ripe Peaches

1 cup halved Green Grapes

1 cup halved Red Grapes

Thinly slice fruits and combine everything in a pitcher. Refrigerate overnight. Add a few ice cubes to each glass before serving.

♈ Kiwi Carnival

¼ cup (2 oz) fresh Kiwi Juice (1 oz in a smaller flute glass)

2 tsp Lemon Juice (1 tsp in a flute)

6 counts Agave Syrup (3 in a flute)

Champagne or White Wine

1 COUNT
agave SYRUP
= a 1-second
SQUIRT
see page 15

Stir juices and agave syrup in a chilled wine glass or flute and add wine or champagne. Garnish with a kiwi wheel.

🍶 Kiwi Sangria

2 bottles Pinot Noir red wine

2 inches Fresh Ginger root, sliced thin

4 Kiwis, peeled and sliced into wheels

1 Tbsp Lime Juice

Peel or scrub the ginger root and then thinly slice it with a mandoline or sharp knife. Combine everything together in a pitcher and refrigerate overnight. Add a few ice cubes to each glass before serving.

Deep Red

½ cup (4 oz) Red Wine

½ cup (4 oz) Orange Juice

1 Tbsp Black Cherry Juice

4 counts Agave Syrup

Shake lightly with ice, or stir then add ice. Strain into a chilled wine glass, adding a few of the ice cubes to the glass. Garnish with an orange slice.

Jamaican Cooler

½ cup (4 oz) Red Wine

½ cup (4 oz) Orange Juice

Splash (1 oz) Lemon or Lime Juice

6 counts Agave Syrup

25 drops (1/8 tsp) Jamaican Rum Spice or a dash of Allspice

Shake lightly with 2 cups of ice, or stir then add ice. Serve in a hurricane glass. Garnish with an orange wheel.

Sangria

2 bottles dry Red or White Wine

½ each sliced Orange, Lemon and Lime

1 cup Orange Juice

¼ cup (2 oz) Agave Syrup

Thinly slice fruits and combine everything in a pitcher. Refrigerate overnight. Add a few ice cubes to each glass before serving.

Chapter 6
Fresh Party Occasions & Themes

"I thought my life would seem more interesting with a musical score and a laugh track." - Bill Watterson

When planning a Fresh Party, choose an occasion that won't interfere with typical junk food events, like birthdays (cake and ice cream) and the Super Bowl (pizza and beer), although I have included a nutty birthday cake recipe on page 100, for those who are game. Instead, focus on introducing **new traditions** to your circle of family and friends. Consider options from this chapter and personalize them according to your tastes, interests and location.

Besides the suggestions for Fresh Party occasions on the following page, you can easily create a Theme Party using the drink and food recipes in this book. Consider one of these:

Hawaiian Luau
Pirate/Caribbean
Jungle/Tarzan
Garden of Eden
Mardi Gras
Mexican Fiesta
Red Hat
Big City Brunch
Greek/Toga

Seasonal Occasions

Planting Party – Gather your friends together to create a garden.

Fruit Party – Choose a specific fruit that comes into season for a short time, like strawberries, cherries, peaches, figs, etc.

Harvest Party – Focus on apples and pears, and plan it in October to include a pumpkin carving contest.

Garden Party – When your flowers bloom, celebrate!

TV Event – Rather than a rowdy occasion, choose an inspiring event like the Olympics, or a marathon or tennis tournament.

A Housewarming or Birthday celebration for yourself or another friend who's excited about juices and won't miss the junk food.

Special Party Favors

Spa Day – Invite someone to give facial treatments, massages or foot soaks to your Fresh Party guests.

Kombucha or Cider Making – Teach your guests something new and send them home with a tasty gift.

Wine Tasting – Get an expert to talk about wines, or get a wine book for beginners and learn the lingo together.

Support Local Music – Invite a local musician to serenade your guests.

Psychic Party – Tarot, palm and skull readings are especially fun.

Guided Meditation – Relax your guests and get them in the spirit of a Fresh Party with an inspiring visualization.

Game or Tournament – Consider lawn games, like croquet, as well as card or board games, including a tournament.

Picnic or Beach Party – Natural settings can inspire people to enjoy fresh and raw foods even more.

Hawaiian Luau

Capture the essence of the Hawaiian islands with pineapples and tropical fruits, macadamia nuts and nori seaweed. Decorate with whole pineapples, colorful flowers, tiki torches, and maybe some fake birds. Find some Hawaiian-style music and learn the hula together. Make sure you have a lei for each of your guests, and flowers for their hair. If you're really into seaweed, offer tastes of different kinds for your guests, and serve Bloody Caesars with seaweed flakes.

Drinks

Bloody Caesar (see Bloody Mary)

Pacific Islander

Fresh Hurricane

Piña Colada

Pacific Cruise

Captain's Cocktail

Kiwi Sangria

Food

Fresh pineapple, mango and papaya

Fresh macadamia nuts

Tropical Fruit Dip

Carob Spice Cashews

Nori Crunchies

Macadamia Chocolate Chip Bites

Pirate/Caribbean

The possibilities for this theme are endless! Listen to a Pirates of the Caribbean CD, or reggae or steel drum music. Eye patches and bandanas are a must. Serve the drinks in coconut shells or old glass bottles. Decorate with coconuts and bowls or bags of citrus fruits, and have lots of lime wedges cut up and available.

"Life's pretty good, and why wouldn't it be? I'm a pirate, after all." - Johnny Depp

Drinks

Pacific Islander

Island Splash

Fresh Hurricane

Coco Mojito

Mai Tai

Hot Jamaican

Pineapple Margarita

Caribbean Cocktail

Food

Fresh pineapple, mango and papaya

Fresh macadamia and Brazil nuts

Tough young coconut meat pieces

Caribbean Lime Fruit Dip

Chili Lime Pistachios

Blimey Bites

Jungle/Tarzan

Tarzan costumes can be sexy and fun, and a Jungle Book theme can be great for small children. In fact, you can play an old Tarzan movie or the Jungle Book during the party. Play a CD featuring dramatic drumming, or supply drums for your guests to play. Buy a case of bananas and hang bunches everywhere, giving them to your guests to take home afterward.

Drinks

Deep Forest Freeze

Tropical Sunrise

Swinging Ape

Skittle

Flying Monkey

Banana Banshee

Aztec Gold

Kombucha Cooler

Food

Fresh bananas and mango

Fresh Brazil nuts or mixed nuts

Chimp's Treat roll-ups

Tropical Fruit Dip

Carob Spice Cashews

Tropical Bites

Garden of Eden

This Fresh Party can be sincere or kitschy, depending on your crowd. Find some decorations or place mats shaped like large leaves and invite guests to attach them to the outside of their clothing or bathing suits. Create a centerpiece, like a tree in your yard full of rubber snakes. Encourage guests to draw pictures or make collages of their visions of Paradise. This would be a great occasion for a guided meditation or spiritual reading.

> *"And God said, Behold, I have given you every herb bearing seed, which is upon the face of all the earth, and every tree, in the which is the fruit of a tree yielding seed; to you it shall be for meat." - Genesis 1:29, King James Bible*

Drinks

Poolside Freeze

Sour Apple

Tree Climber

Apple Colada

Cherry Martini

Wine Cooler

Food

Fresh tree fruits – apples, pears, peaches, cherries

Fresh almonds and pecans, or mixed nuts in the shell

Caramel Apples

Peachy Mint Fruit Dip

Cinnamon Pecans

Berry Apple Bites

Mardi Gras

February, after the worst of winter, is the perfect time for a long fast. But before the fast, a fabulous celebration is at hand! "Fat Tuesday," the day before Lent begins, is the third and last day of Mardi Gras. It is both a celebration of having survived the winter and a fertility festival for the coming spring, just forty days away.

Celebrate with decor, masks and beads for all your guests in the Mardi Gras colors: gold, green and purple. Listen to some jazz music too, in the spirit of New Orleans.

Drinks

Peach Daiquiri

Bayou Sunset

Southern Breeze

Swamp Water

Georgia Tea

Banana Boat

Grasshopper

Kiwi Sangria

Food

Fresh peaches, apricots and oranges

Fresh almonds and pecans

Peach Mint Fruit Dip

Carob Spice Cashews

Peach Ice Dream

Orange Pecan Bites

Mexican Fiesta

Celebrate the vivid colors and flavors of our southern neighbor with your own Fresh Fiesta. Find some Mexican party music, learn a group dance, smack a piñata filled with nuts in the shell, and let the limes, agave and raw cacao flow!

Decorate with bright colors, and have maracas within reach. Hang batches of chili peppers (real or fake) from the rafters.

Drinks

Margaritas of all kinds

Island Splash

Coco Mojito

Banana Java

Bob Marley

Banana Banshee

Frozen Matador

Sangria

Food

Fresh bananas, mangos and papaya

Fresh mixed nuts in the shell in a piñata

Arriba Salsa & Guacamole

Spicy Herb Crackers

Chili Lime Pistachios

Jalapeno Poppers

Red Hat

Red and pink are the colors of the day! Make all your decor, flowers, drinks and food reflect these most festive and eye-catching of colors. The mood is vibrant, outrageous and feminine, no matter who your guests are - think of old-fashioned parlors, salons and tea rooms. If you have lace table covers and curtains, and a frilly tea set, bring them out for the occasion. For music, play something classical and upbeat, like Chopin.

Drinks

Strawberry Bash

Fourth of July

Coco-Berry Freeze

Bouncing Cherry

Red Hat Cocktail

Pink Lemonade

Boston Tea

Food

Fresh mixed berries, red grapes and apples

Assorted aged cheeses

Berry Mint Fruit Dip

Paprika Ricotta Hors d'oeuvre

Sun-dried Tomato Sunflower Pate

Fresh Herb Crackers

Berry Apple Bites

Big City Brunch

A big city brunch is a refined affair. Familiar brunch drinks include the traditional Bloody Mary, as well as champagne drinks like mimosas and kirs, and the food is generally on the rich side. Decorate with fresh exotic flowers; use nice tablecloths and cloth napkins; and garnish your drinks to the max! For music, go with New Age (like Enya), or play techno dance music to keep the party going.

Drinks

Real Bloody Mary/Caesar

Harvey Wallbanger

Honeydew Cocktail

Dance the Night Away

Spanish Coffee

Cosmopolitan

Mimosa

Kir Royale

Food

Fresh melons and strawberries

Fresh mixed nuts

Assorted aged cheeses, including brie

Berry Mint Fruit Dip

Paprika Ricotta Hors d'oeuvre

Cinnamon Pecans

Berry Apple Bites

Greek/Toga

White sheets and sandals - what more does a Toga Party need? Head garlands, bunches of grapes, and sweet licorice-flavored drinks (as a tribute to Ouzo), for starters. Greek music is raucous, so spontaneous dancing and plate smashing might ensue. Set up a gourmet olive bar or a wine tasting. Read a passage from Homer or Plato. Yell "Opa!" when anything happens at all.

Drinks

Ginger Apple Sour

Good & Plenty

Heavenly Spirits

Jaguar

Seaside Cooler

Sangria Blanca

Food

Grapes, apples, figs and olives

Caramel Apples

Fresh almonds and walnuts

Assorted aged cheeses, including goat cheese

Walnut Tapenade Dip

Stuffed Grape Leaves

Fresh Herb Crackers

Lemon Garlic Almonds

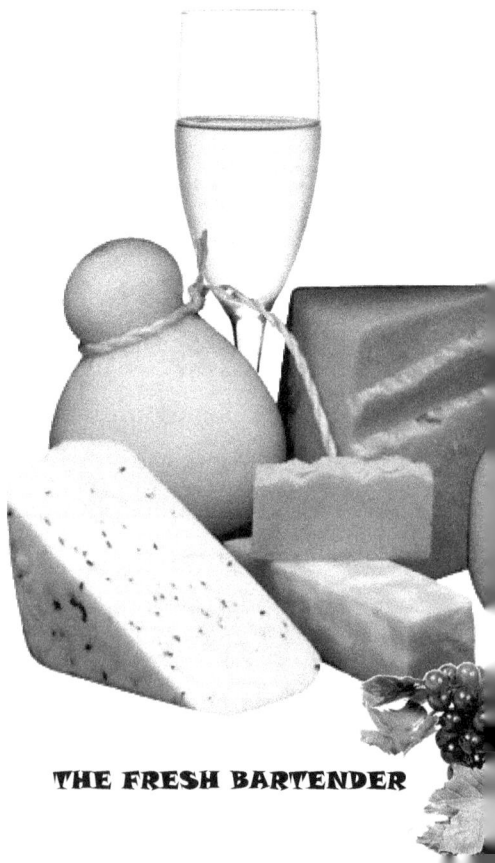

Chapter 7
Fresh Party
Platters
& Munchies

*"I like nonsense, it wakes up
the brain cells." - Dr. Seuss*

Keeping with the spirit of fresh, high-enzyme foods, this chapter is full of options for flavorful party snacks, from simple fruit dips and flavored nuts to "live" versions of Jalapeno Poppers and nutty birthday cakes.

See the following page for no-fuss party platter ideas, or explore some innovative treats from the annals of gourmet raw foods. For convenience, I've included dairy options where appropriate. What's important is that you have as much fun preparing for the party as you will have hosting it.

The previous chapter, on Theme Parties, can help you to organize your menu and make planning your Fresh Party more manageable.

Chimp's Treat Roll-ups

Whole peeled Bananas

Mango slices and pineapple cut into thin strips

Orange or lemon zest (optional)

Large leafy greens like chard or lacinto kale

Chimpanzees are known to roll a banana (usually unpeeled!) into a large leaf and eat it burrito-style, but for us humans, some added mango or pineapple and a dash of zest will make it much more exciting.

No-fuss Fruit

Tropical Fruit – A tropical ambience is relaxing and vacation-like, so serve fresh pineapple, mango and papaya. Bunches of bananas, as well as whole pineapples, can serve as decor.

Northern Fruit – These familiar, tasty fruits grow in the North: apples, pears, berries, cherries and melons. Apples and pears can be sliced ahead and tossed with lemon juice to reduce browning.

Seasonal Fruit – An occasion can easily be made for fruit that has a short growing season or specific harvest time, like berries, cherries and figs, or apples for the cider-making season.

Regional Fruit – When throwing a Theme Party (see previous chapter), serve fresh fruit that is region-specific, like grapes, olives and figs for Greece, and mango and banana for Mexico.

No-fuss Nuts

Nuts in the Shell – Cracking fresh nuts is a familiar party activity. Filling a piñata with nuts in the shell is fun, whether you're creating a Mexican theme, celebrating a birthday, or expecting children.

Shelled Nuts – Once nuts are shelled, they can go rancid quickly, so purchase them from a trusted source and keep them in the refrigerator until the Fresh Party date.

No-fuss Cheeses

Aged Cheeses – Serve your Fresh Party guests only the best: cheeses that have been aged 100 days or more. Aged cheeses contain no lactose, and they're rich in enzymes. These cheeses should be clearly labeled, since the manufacturers *want* you to know they're aged – it puts them in the "gourmet" category. The sharper the cheddar, the more likely it'll be aged. Goat cheese is also considered an optimally digestible gourmet cheese.

Arriba Salsa

3 medium Tomatoes, finely chopped

4 Tbsp Lemon or Lime Juice

1 Jalapeno, seeded and minced

1/3 cup Onion, chopped

½ tsp Sea Salt

Stir everything together and marinate for 30-60 minutes. Serve with fresh zucchini and carrot "chip" rounds, and flax crackers or chips.

Arriba Guacamole

Make a batch of salsa. Mash 3 avocados with a little juice from the salsa, and then stir salsa and mashed avocado together. Stir in 2 Tbsp pine nuts or pepitas (pumpkin seeds).

Fruit Dip Bases

Base # 1: Blend 2 ripe bananas with 1 avocado

Base #2: Blend 1 cup cashews (soaked 8-12 hours and rinsed) with 4-6 pitted dates, soaked 30 minutes in ½ cup water (use the water also), and 1 tsp vanilla or almond extract

Base #3: 1 ½ cups vanilla yogurt

Blend the Fruit Dip Base of your choice with the ingredients listed in one of the recipes on the following page. Serve with a platter of bite-sized pieces or slices of fruit.

Tropical Fruit Dip

Fruit Dip Base

½ cup frozen Pineapple

½ cup frozen Mango

1 Tbsp Lime Juice

Caribbean Lime Fruit Dip

Fruit Dip Base

½ cup frozen Pineapple

½ cup soft young Coconut meat

2 Tbsp Lime Juice

Peach Mint Fruit Dip

Fruit Dip Base

1 cup frozen Peaches

1 Tbsp Lemon Juice

8-10 leaves fresh Mint (add last and pulse blend)

Berry Mint Fruit Dip

Fruit Dip Base

1 cup frozen Mixed Berries

1 Tbsp Lemon Juice

8-10 leaves fresh Mint (add last)

Walnut Tapenade Dip

1 cup Walnuts, soaked 30 min. (can substitute ½ Pine Nuts)

½ cup raw sesame Tahini

¼ cup Lemon Juice

¼ cup cold-pressed Olive Oil

2 cloves Garlic, or ¼ tsp dried

30 small black or 24 kalamata Olives, pitted

2 cups chopped Parsley

½ cup chopped Red Onion

¼ cup chopped fresh Basil, or ½ tsp dried

In a food processor or blender, puree nuts, tahini, oil, lemon juice and garlic until smooth, adding water as necessary. Add the rest of the ingredients and pulse blend. Serve as a dip for veggies or flax crackers, or as hors d oeuvres atop zucchini rounds or crackers.

Sun-dried Tomato Sunflower Pate

Soak 1 ½ cups raw sunflower seeds in water for 8-12 hours and substitute them for the nuts in the recipe above. Omit the olives. Soak ½ cup sun-dried tomatoes in water for 15-30 minutes, then chop and pulse blend into the dip.

Stuffed Grape Leaves

Buy a jar of whole grape leaves, and pat two dozen of them dry with a paper towel. Wrap each leaf around a dollop of Walnut Tapenade Dip or Sunflower Pate with some chopped cucumber. Arrange on a plate with the seams on the bottom. *"OPA!"*

Creamy Spinach Dip

4 cups Spinach, chopped

½ cup Onion, minced

½ cup Red Bell Pepper, minced

3 Tbsp Lemon Juice

2 Tbsp Olive Oil

1 tsp Sea Salt

1 cup raw Cashews, soaked

½ cup Pine Nuts or Cashews, soaked

1 stalk Celery, chopped

2 Tbsp Lemon Juice

½ tsp Nutmeg

¼ tsp each Cayenne and Black Pepper

Marinate the spinach, onion and bell pepper in the lemon juice, olive oil and salt for 30-60 minutes, or until the spinach has softened and reduced. In the meantime, soak the cashews and pine nuts in water for 30 minutes.

Drain the nuts, saving the soak water. In a blender or Vita-Mix, blend the stalk of celery with the 2 Tb additional lemon juice, all of the excess spinach marinade, and a little soak water. Add the nuts and puree until smooth, coaching the mixture with a spatula from the top if necessary. Mix the spices into the creamy dip by hand, and then add the marinated spinach, onion and pepper. Chill before serving, if possible.

Serve with a variety of dippin' veggies.

Cinnamon Pecans

3 cups raw Pecans, soaked in water 8-12 hours and rinsed

¼ cup Maple Syrup or Agave Syrup

2 Tbsp Cinnamon

Toss the nuts with syrup until well coated, then add spices and stir. Dehydrate at 110° for 1-2 hours on a solid dehydrator sheet and then 3-4 hours longer on a mesh sheet.

Carob Spice Cashews

Follow the above recipe, using cashews. Reduce the cinnamon to 2 tsp and add 2 Tbsp of carob powder.

Lemon Garlic Almonds

3 cups raw Almonds

¼ cup Nama Shoyu, soy sauce or wheat-free tamari

1 tsp Garlic Powder

1 tsp Lemon Zest

Toss the nuts with tamari until well coated, then add spices and stir. Dehydrate at 110° for 1-2 hours on a solid dehydrator sheet and then 3-4 hours longer on a mesh sheet.

Chili Lime Pistachios

Follow the above recipe, using raw pistachios. Substitute half of the tamari with lime juice and the garlic powder with chili powder. Use lemon or lime zest.

Jalapeno Poppers

Fresh Filling:

1 cup Cashews, soaked 8-12 hours and rinsed

½ cup Pine Nuts, soaked 8-12 hours and rinsed

1 ½ Tbsp Lime or Lemon Juice

2 counts Agave Syrup

1 tsp Sea Salt

1/3 cup chopped Cilantro (add last and pulse blend)

Dairy Filling:

½ package organic Cream Cheese, softened

¾ cup shredded aged Cheddar Cheese

¼ tsp Sea Salt

½ tsp each Lime or Lemon Zest and dried Oregano

Crumble Topping:

¼ cup each Hazelnuts and Sunflower Seeds, crumbled in a food processor, OR Breadcrumbs

Combine filling in a food processor with an S-blade until smooth. Cut about ¾ pound jalapeno peppers lengthwise, remove the seeds and fill each half with filling. Roll in or sprinkle with the topping.

Dehydrate at 110° for 4-6 hours or until soft, OR bake on a greased cookie sheet, uncovered, at 300° for 20-25 minutes.

Orange Pecan Bites

2 cups pitted Dates, more or less

1 cup Orange Juice to soak dates

1 cup Almonds or Hazelnuts

1 cup Pecans

1 tsp Cinnamon

½ Tbsp Orange Zest

To create these finger food Bites, you'll want to create a doughy, yet somewhat dry, consistency, so they'll stand up to being handled.

Soak the dried fruit in fruit juice for 1 hour. In a food processor with an S-blade, crumble the nuts with spices and zest. Add the soaked dates a few pieces at a time until the mixture holds together, then add a splash of juice to create a doughy consistency. If it's too wet to handle, you can mix in some psyllium husk powder or ground flax seeds, which will soak up moisture after some time. Press the mixture into a square container to about ¾-inch thick. Refrigerate for at least a few hours.

Option 1: Cut into bite-sized squares and serve.

Option 2: Roll the squares into balls and dust with cacao or carob powder, cinnamon, dried coconut or crushed nuts.

Option 3: Dehydrate squares for a few hours at 110° to make them easier to handle.

Blimey Bites

Adjust the above recipe by replacing half the dates with dried pineapple, and the orange juice with lime juice. Use a mixture of nuts, including cashews, and add ½ cup dried coconut.

Tropical Bites

Adjust the Orange Pecan Bites recipe by replacing 2/3 of the dates with dried mango. Use a mixture of nuts, including cashews, and add ½ cup dried coconut. Add a whole ripe banana to the mix.

Berry Apple Bites

1 cup pitted Dates

1 cup Dried Apple

1 cup Apple Juice to soak dates and dried apples

½ cup Apple Pulp from juicing (optional)

¾ cup Mixed Berries, fresh or thawed frozen

2 cups total Walnuts and Almonds

1 tsp Cinnamon

Macadamia Chocolate Bites

2 cups pitted Dates

1 cup Orange or Pineapple Juice to soak dates

½ cup Pineapple Pulp from juicing (optional)

2 cups total Macadamias, Cashews and Almonds

½ cup Dried Coconut

½ cup Cacao Nibs OR ¼ cup Cacao Powder

1 tsp Orange Zest

Paprika Ricotta Hors d'oeuvre

2 cups Walnuts or Cashews, soaked 8-12 hours and rinsed

¼ cup Water

2 Tbsp cold-pressed Flax or Sesame Oil

1 Tbsp Nama Shoyu, Soy Sauce or wheat-free Tamari

2 Tbsp Lemon Juice

3 cloves Garlic, crushed, or ¼ tsp dried

½ Tbsp Paprika

¼ cup fresh Mint or Parsley leaves, chopped

Fresh thick Cucumber slices

Paprika and Olives for garnish, if desired

Combine all ingredients except the green herbs in a food processor or blender, until ricotta-like in texture. Add the greens and pulse blend several times, leaving small pieces intact.

To serve, place a dollop of ricotta on a cucumber slice, and top with a sprinkle of paprika and a slice of olive. Alternately, place a dollop on a cracker or piece of flax cracker (see next page).

96

Fresh Herb Crackers

1 cup Flax Seeds, whole

1 cup Flax Seeds, whole or ground

1 ½ cup Water

½ cup raw sesame Tahini at room temperature

1 cup finely chopped fresh herbs - Parsley, Cilantro, Basil

1 clove Garlic

2 Tbsp Nama Shoyu, Soy Sauce or wheat-free Tamari

2 Tbsp Lemon Juice

2 tsp Sea Salt

1 tsp dried Oregano or Italian Seasoning

In a mixing bowl, whisk together the tahini and water. Mix the whole and ground flax seeds in a large bowl and then add all ingredients and stir well. Soak for 30 minutes or until mixture thickens.

Spread the flax mixture on solid dehydrator sheets and dehydrate at 110° for 2-3 hours. Remove the crackers from the solid sheets and dehydrate on mesh sheets for 4 more hours, or until dry (this will depend upon thickness).

Spicy Herb Crackers

Remove tahini from the above recipe, and be sure to use fresh chopped cilantro and dried oregano. Add 2 small finely chopped jalapeno peppers, and allow the mixture to soak for 2-3 hours before dehydrating.

Nori Crunchies

1 cup Flax Seeds

¼ cup raw hulled Sesame Seeds

1 Tbsp Dulse or Kelp Flakes, or Nori pieces

Pinch of Garlic Powder and dried Ginger

½ cup Water

2 Tbsp Nama Shoyu or wheat-free Tamari

1 Tbsp Honey or Agave Syrup

Nori sheets, raw untoasted

Stir together the flax and sesame seeds, seaweed flakes, garlic and ginger. In a separate bowl, whisk together the water, Nama Shoyu and sweetener. Combine and allow to soak for 30 minutes.

With a sharp knife, cut about 3 large nori sheets into 8 pieces each, as shown below. With a pastry brush or your finger, wet each piece of nori thoroughly. Place a small teaspoonful of flax mixture on a nori piece, and wrap. With the seam side down, flatten each piece to about ¼ inch thick. Dehydrate at 110° on mesh dehydrator sheets for 3-4 hours or until crisp.

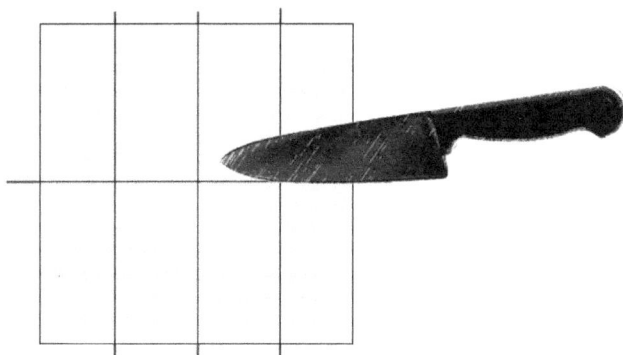

THE FRESH BARTENDER

Fruity Ice Dream

2 cups fresh or thawed frozen fruit - Peaches, Berries, Pineapple, Mango

2 soft ripe Bananas

¼ cup fruit juice of your choice

2 Tbsp sweetener of your choice

¼ cup raw Carob Powder (optional)

Mash all ingredients together with a potato masher or in a food processor.

Freeze for a couple of hours and re-mash. The more often you can mash the mixture as it freezes, the more ice cream-like it will be. An ice cream maker works well too. Freeze to desired consistency and enjoy.

Creamy Ice Dream

Blend 1/2 cup cashews or young coconut meat with 1 cup juice or coconut water, and then add the fruit and sweetener, doubling the sweetener to 4 Tbsp. Follow the directions above.

Chocolate Sauce

In a blender, combine 2 cups maple syrup with ¼ cup cold-pressed coconut or olive oil, and 2/3 cup raw cacao or carob powder.

Nutty Birthday Cake

1 cup raw Buckwheat Groats

1 cup Almonds, soaked 8-12 hours and rinsed

½ cup raw Cashews or Walnuts

¼ cup Lemon Juice

¼ cup Lemon Zest

¼ cup Agave Syrup or pure Honey

1 ½ cups pitted chopped Dates

First, create a sprouted buckwheat flour by soaking the groats in water for 5-6 hours and then dehydrating at less than 118° for 12-16 hours or until dry. Grind to a coarse flour in a coffee grinder.

Combine the nuts in a food processor with an S-blade until crumbled. Add the lemon, sweetener and dates. Add the buckwheat flour last, and after combining, remove from the processor immediately and shape into a cake about 1 ¼ inches thick.

Chocolate Birthday Cake

In the above recipe, omit the lemon, and add 1 ½ Tbsp vanilla extract and a little water, if necessary to moisten. Mix 3 Tbsp raw cacao powder with the buckwheat flour before adding.

Vanilla Cream Topping

In a blender, combine 1 cup raw cashews (soaked at least 30 minutes) with 6 pitted dates, 2 Tbsp agave syrup or raw honey, and ½ of a vanilla bean. Blend until very smooth, adding water or coconut water to thin, if needed to blend. Spread atop the Nutty Cake and top with chopped nuts.

Caramel Apples

2 cups Dates (about 18 large), pitted

1/3 cup pure Honey

6 to 8 small tart Apples

Ground or chopped raw Almonds, Hazelnuts, Pecans or Walnuts, or a mixture (optional)

Soak the dates in water for 30 to 60 minutes and then drain. (Save the soak water - it's great in smoothies!) Puree the dates and honey until smooth. If using a VitaMix or food processor, use 1/3 cup honey; you can use more if using a regular kitchen blender.

Option 1: Slice apples and use the puree as a dip. Coat apple slices with a little lemon juice to prevent browning.

Option 2: Spread each whole apple with a thin layer of puree, and then sprinkle with nuts. Insert popsicle sticks to use as handles.

Appendix I
Making Kombucha

So, you're ready to start fermenting on your own! Making kombucha at home is cheap and easy, once you learn to use and store the "mother" and "child" cultures. If you know you want to keep kombucha around and serve it to your Fresh Party guests, there's no better way than to make it yourself.

Purchase a kombucha "mother" culture from a source online or in the Resources section of this book. For more detailed photos and instructions, search the internet or purchase a good how-to book, like *Wild Fermentation* by Sandor Ellix Katz. You may also be able to get information from Asian markets or health food stores in your area. Ask around - you never know who may have kombucha growing in their kitchens!

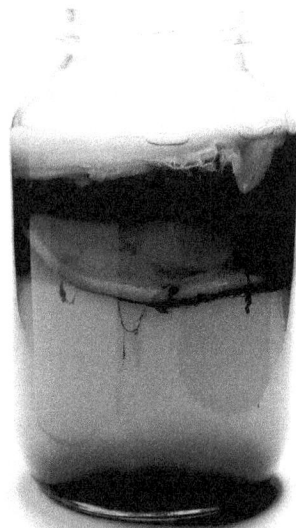

Kombucha Tea

2 quarts filtered water

1/2 cup white sugar

2 tablespoons loose black tea or 4 tea bags

1 cup mature acidic Kombucha

Kombucha "mother" culture

Mix water and sugar and bring to a boil in a small pot., then turn off the heat, add tea, cover and steep about 15 minutes. Strain tea (if loose) into a glass container. Allow tea to cool to body temperature (warmer than skin temperature). Add mature acidic Kombucha. (When you obtain a culture, it will be stored in this liquid.) Place the Kombucha mother culture in the container. Cover it with a clean cloth and store in a clean, warm spot, ideally 70 to 85 degrees, undisturbed.

After a few days to one week, depending on temperature, you will notice a skin forming on the surface of the mixture. The kombucha will continue to get more acidic and less sweet the longer it sits. You can decide the kombucha is done simply by your own taste, or you can use pH strips to check for a level around 3 pH.

You can stop the fermentation by cooling your kombucha tea in the refrigerator, but first you must start your next batch or store your mother culture in the refrigerator with about 8 ounces of your new kombucha tea.

You now have the original culture you started with, and a "child," the skin that formed on your new batch. Use either the mother or child culture for your next batch, and pass the other one on to a friend. You've just recaptured the excitement of childhood science experiments!

See "Flavored Kombucha" Recipes on page 105

Anna Bielecki (left) of Nature's Wisdom Bistro - expert maker of kombucha, mulled wine and many other delicacies.

Anna's Kombucha Tips

- Stainless steel pots are best; don't use aluminum.

- Use plastic utensils only, not metal. If you use wooden utensils, make sure they're clean and bacteria-free.

- Get creative with the tea blends you use.

- You can make several gallons at once. Simply use a large pot and strain the sweetened tea into smaller containers. Use a 3- to 4-inch piece of kombucha culture per gallon container.

- When the kombucha is sour enough for you, then it's done.

- You can add small pieces of your leftover cultures to your smoothies!

Flavored Kombucha

You can flavor kombucha in two ways:

First, you can use different kinds of tea bags in your original mixture, though it's recommended to use some black tea. For instance, you can use 2 black tea bags, 2 green tea bags and 2 flavored herbal tea bags all together, or 2 black tea bags and 4 flavored bags.

Second, you can add juice to your kombucha after it's made.

Anna's Special – Use 3 rooibos (red bush), 1 fenugreek and 2 echinacea tea bags to make the kombucha.

Lemon Green Kombucha – Use 2 black tea bags, 2 green tea bags and 2 lemon herbal tea bags (or 4 lemon green tea bags). Mix fresh lemon juice with the kombucha after it's fermented.

Chinese Orange – Use 4 oolong and 2 mint tea bags in the kombucha, and mix with fresh orange juice or orange juice concentrate.

Apple Ginger – Use 2 oolong and 4 apple cinnamon tea bags to make the kombucha, then add fresh ginger juice afterward.

Elderberry Cherry – Use 2 black tea and 4 elderberry tea bags in the kombucha, and add Black Cherry Rejuvenate after fermentation.

Tropical Spice – Make the kombucha with 4 black and 2 chai tea bags, and then add fresh pineapple juice or a tropical juice concentrate after fermenting.

Blackcurrant and Rose Hip – Boil 8 Tbsp dried rose hips in 2 quarts of water in a covered pot for 10 minutes before stirring in the sugar and steeping the tea bags - use 2 black tea and 4 blackcurrant flavored tea bags. Add Black Cherry Rejuvenate after fermenting, if desired.

Rooibos Vanilla – Use 6 vanilla-flavored rooibos (red bush) tea bags to make the kombucha.

Appendix II
Traditional Liquors

"I feel sorry for people who don't drink. When they wake up in the morning, that's as good as they're going to feel all day." - Frank Sinatra

Depending on the makeup of your Fresh Party crowd, you may want to have some traditional liquors on hand. You are offering fabulously fresh juices, which are a luxury with and without alcohol. If you choose only one from the list below, make it rum, or a sweet-flavored cordial. *Note:* "80 proof" means 40% alcohol.

Brandy is distilled from mashed grapes or other fruit, aged in oak casks, and bottled at 80 or 84 proof. It is usually sipped by itself but is also an ingredient in Spanish Coffee and Brandy Alexander. **Cognac** is a smooth brandy from the Cognac region of France.

Gin is distilled from grain, and each brand uses unique flavors from juniper berries and other botanicals. It is bottled between 80 and 94 proof. It is the traditional martini base.

Rum is distilled from fermented sugar cane and molasses and bottled at no less than 80 proof. It is most often used with tropical juices and coconut. **Dark Rum** is heavier, sweeter and more pungent. **Jamaican Rum** is traditionally flavored with allspice, chilis and vanilla.

Tequila is distilled from the blue agave plant in Mexico and is bottled between 76 and 92 proof. It is the primary liquor (with Triple Sec) in margaritas.

Vodka can be distilled from potatoes, corn, wheat and other grains, and is bottled between 80 and 110 proof. It is filtered and refined to have an "invisible" flavor and aroma. It is used in a wide variety of drinks and is the modern martini base preference.

Whiskey is distilled from a fermented mash of grain (corn, rye, barley, wheat, etc.), aged in oak barrels and bottled at no less than 80 proof. It is most commonly drunk by itself or with a mild mixer like soda water, or as a Whiskey Sour. *Bourbon* is a whiskey distilled from a mash containing at least half corn. *Scotch* is a whiskey made only in Scotland from a mash including malted barley dried over peat fires, giving it a distinctive smoky flavor.

Sweet Cordials

Amaretto is a brand of almond-flavored liqueur.

Chambord is flavored with black raspberries and is an ingredient of a Kir Royale (with champagne).

Creme de Banana is a banana-flavored liqueur.

Creme de Cacao is a clear or brown-colored, cacao-flavored liqueur and an ingredient in a Grasshopper (with Creme de Menthe).

Creme de Menthe is clear or green-colored, and mint-flavored.

Frangelico is a brand of hazelnut-flavored liqueur.

Irish Cream is a creamy liqueur based on whiskey and coffee. Bailey's is the best-known producer.

Kahlua is a brand of coffee-flavored liqueur and is the principal ingredient in Black and White Russians.

Midori is bright green and melon-flavored.

Triple Sec is an orange-flavored liqueur used in margaritas, Spanish Coffees and many other popular drinks. *Curacao* is like Triple Sec, but is colored bright blue or red.

Appendix III
Set Up A Fresh Bar

"If it's not fun, you're not doing it right." - Bob Basso

Setting up your Fresh Bar like a pro will help your guests feel festive, carefree and well taken care of. A nice set up for your bar will communicate your intention to go all out for your loved ones to ensure a good time for everyone. You, as the host, will be setting the stage for exactly the atmosphere you want - one of love and good cheer.

I have included only the basics here, including the glassware I recommend for this book and a discussion of juicers. See pages 114 and 115 for more photos of the equipment in action.

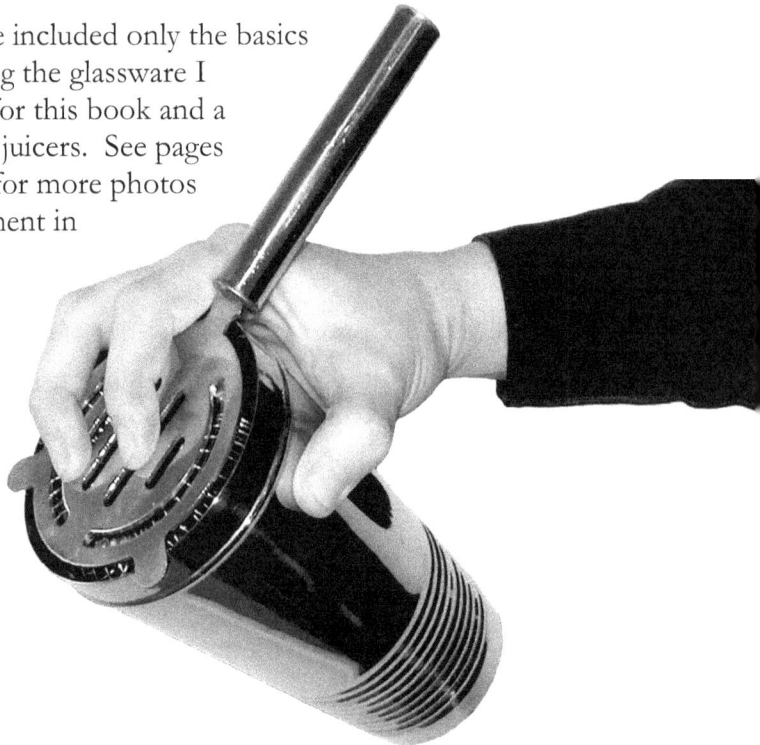

THE FRESH BARTENDER

Shake it like the pros!

I bought a pint beer glass for a dollar at a resale shop so I could "shake it" at home like I did when I was a pro. Buy a thick glass with a nice round edge, so it'll be strong enough for shaking ice and will create a secure seal. Cock the glass to one side on top of your shaker so it doesn't get stuck. Shaking brightly colored drinks creates the perfect sights and sounds for a festive party! The opposite page shows how the strainer sits in the shaker cup.

Fresh Bar Equipment

Blender

Shaker

Strainer

Ice Scoop

Jigger

Muddler

Garnish Caddy

Store-n-Pour
Containers

Napkins, Straws
& Caddy

Optional: You'll need a nylon **nut milk bag** if you'll be making fresh nut creams from hard nuts like almonds and hazelnuts. See page 40 for recipes.

Blender - A Vita-Mix or a heavy duty blender made to crush ice will be most useful in your Fresh Bar. A regular household blender will handle a small amount of ice, or ice that's already crushed - or simply use more frozen fruit.

Shaker - The one thing that will give a flourish to your presentation! Shake drinks with ice and then serve in a large hurricane or highball glass, or strain chilled into a martini or cocktail glass. The pros use the shaker cup with a thick pint-sized glass cocked on top of it, instead of the shaker top, which tends to get stuck.

Strainer - Use this to strain drinks from your shaker. The shaker will probably have a lid with strainer holes on top, but these are very slow and will get clogged with muddled fruit or pulp. See the image on page 108 for how to use a strainer with a shaker cup.

Ice Scoop - Choose one that's between 8 and 12 ounces. A must-have at a Fresh Party; tongs are too slow.

Jigger - What every bartender uses, and you'll use to measure intense juices like citrus, cherry, etc. For this book, you'll need jiggers in two sizes: ¾/1 ½ ounces and 1/2 ounces (referring to the small and large ends). The recipes also include tablespoon measures.

Muddler - The muddler will distinguish your Fresh Bar. You'll be able to easily crush mint leaves as well as fragile fruits like watermelon, honeydew, strawberries and banana slices, with abandon!

Garnish Caddy - Keep your garnishes handy with a caddy. The convenient flip-top lid will help keep flies away from the fruit.

Stor-N-Pour (or Flow-n-Stow, etc.) - Keep juices stored in the bottom half with the lid, and then attach the pour top when needed. Sink the whole sturdy container into a bin of ice to keep it cold.

Napkins & Straws Caddy - Keeps them dry and handy.

Nut Milk Bag - Use a nylon mesh bag for creating fresh nut creams from almonds and hazelnuts. For sources, see page 117.

Glasses

Dramatic glasses will help you create a Fresh Party atmosphere. A hurricane glass can turn an ordinary smoothie into a festive treat. Cocktail glasses are for sipping strongly flavored drinks, and thick-bottomed highballs are best for muddling. The recipes in this book have been created specifically for glasses of the following volumes, so you can make adjustments where necessary.

Martini Glass
9 oz.
Chilled drinks
without ice

Cocktail Glass
4.5 oz.
Rich or intense drinks
without ice

Highball Glass
9 oz.
Drinks with ice
Best for muddling

Hurricane Glass
15 oz.
Fancy drinks with
ice or blended

Wine Glass
11oz.
Wine drinks
Mimosa, Kir

Pitcher
64-100 oz.
Punches & margaritas
Party sized batches

THE FRESH BARTENDER

Juicers

You don't have to own a big juicer in order to throw a happening Fresh Party, but a juicer like the two shown below will be necessary to make fresh juices from pineapple, apple, melon, etc. There are two types of juicers for non-citrus fruits:

· **Centrifugal Juicers** use cutting blades and a spinning strainer basket
· **Masticating or Triturating Juicers** mash the vegetables using rotating augers

The nutritional quality of juice from a masticating (single auger) or triturating (double auger) juicer will be superior, especially if the juice is not drunk immediately, but the centrifugal juicers work much faster, which is why they're used in retail juice bars. Furthermore, centrifugal juicers don't work well with leafy greens, since the centrifugal force shoots the leaves directly into the pulp basket, without ever coming into contact with the cutting blades. Centrifugal juicers are also more time-consuming to clean because of the tiny holes in the strainer basket that require a small brush to clear.

A small centrifugal juicer   *A masticating (single auger) juicer*

Above: Use the wide part of a knife or the back corner of a cleaver to open a young coconut. *Left:* Rub a twist of citrus peel around the rim of a glass for flavor. *Below:* A simple corkscrew uses leverage to pull a wine bottle cork.

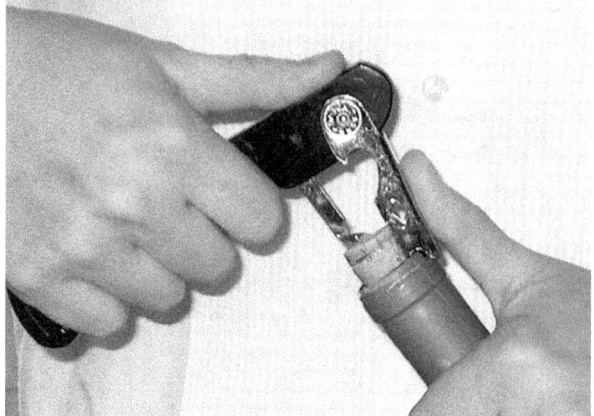

THE FRESH BARTENDER

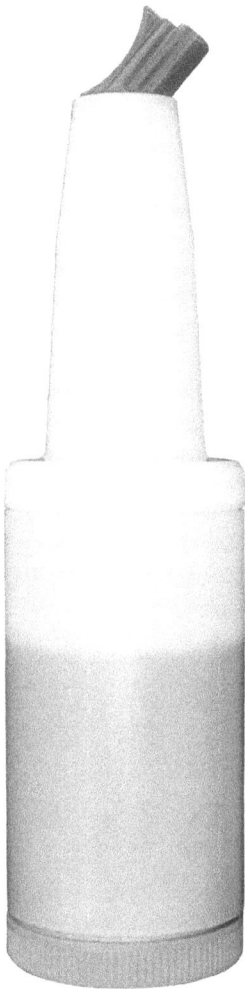

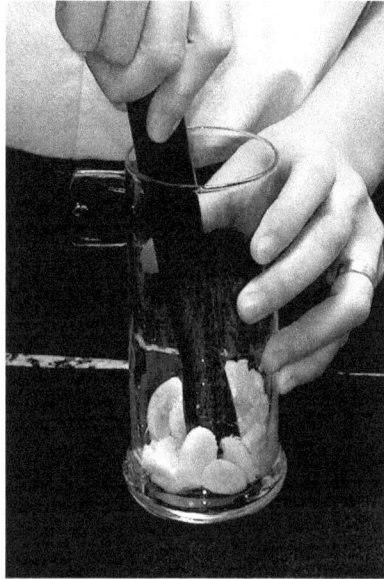

Above: Muddle banana slices in a thick-bottomed glass. *Left:* A Stor-N-Pour juice container with spout. *Below:* Making almond cream with a nylon nut milk bag.

Resources

Bartending Guides

Old Mr. Boston DeLuxe Official Bartender's Guide (Boston: Mr Boston Distiller Corp., 1935-1971...)

The Bartender's Guide by Peter Bohrmann (London: Salamander Books, 1999)

Bartending for Dummies by Ray Foley (Hoboken, NJ: Wiley Publishing, 2003)

Bar Equipment Online

www.kegworks.com 1-877-636-3673

www.barsupplies.com 1-800-Bloody Mary (256-6396)

www.newyorkbarstore.com 1-888-707-4504

Wine & Supplies

www.wineofthemonthclub.com 1-800-949-WINE

www.carljungwines.com (724) 468-4559 - alcohol-free wine

www.wiederkehrwines.com 1-800-622-WINE - alcohol-free wine

www.arielvineyards.com (408) 288-5057 - alcohol-free wine

www.vineguyproductions.com (707) 473-0492 - videos

www.eckraus.com 1-800-353-1906 - home wine making supplies

www.midwestsupplies.com 1-888-449-BREW - wine making

Book - *Wine for Dummies* by McCarthy & Ewing-Mulligan (Foster City, CA: IDG Books Worldwide, 1998)

Juicing Books

Power Juices Super Drinks by Steve Meyerowitz (New York: Kensington Publishing, 2000)

Total Juicing by Elaine LaLanne with Richard Benyo (New York: Penguin Books, 1992)

The Juiceman's Power of Juicing by Jay Kordich

Living with Green Star by Elysa Markowitz

Kombucha Making

www.kombucha.org (315) 267-6769 - cultures and starter kits

www.kombuchacultures.com - info, books and cultures

www.gtskombucha.com 1-877-RE-JUICE - kombucha for retailers

Book - *Wild Fermentation* by Sandor Ellix Katz

Food, Spices & Equipment

www.sunfood.com 1-888-RAW-FOOD - cacao, agave, nuts, juicers

www.madhavasagave.com (303) 823-5166 - agave syrup and honey

www.livingtreecommunity.com 1-800-260-5534 - nuts, honey

www.therawdiet.com (503) 771-3904 - nut milk bags, juicers

www.bestjuicers.com (619) 838-3151 - juicers, blenders

www.spicebarn.com 1-866-670-9040 - Jamaican Rum Spice, vanilla beans, cinnamon, extracts

www.mountainroseherbs.com 1-800-879-3337 - vanilla beans, teas, empty bottles and glass droppers, liquid lecithin

www.naturalhealthyconcepts.com 1-866-505-7501 - get **Premier Research Labs** products - Black Cherry & Pomegranate Rejuvenate, Premier Coffee; flax seeds, energy bars, high quality oils.

Other Titles by Jordan Maerin

*Raw Foods for Busy People: Simple and Machine-Free
Recipes for Every Day
Alimentos Crudos para La Gente Ocupada
Raw Foods for Busy People 2: Green Magic
Raw Foods for Busy People English/Japanese DVD*

EatFreshNow.com

Make it simple. Make it fresh. Make it Now!
Eatfreshnow.com is Jordan's *new* homepage
Featuring quick links, original articles, free sample recipes,
tips for raw food beginners and *video demos!*
Plus a *Free CD*: How to Balance Your Diet

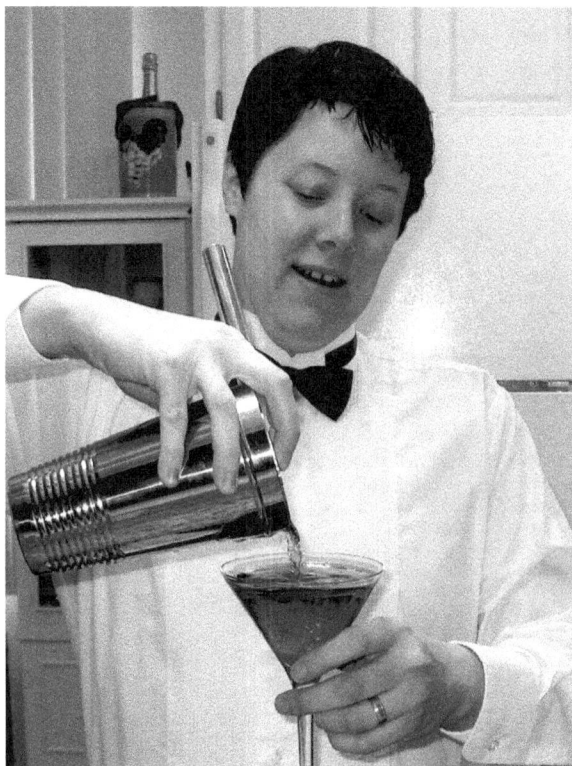

About the Author

Jordan Maerin holds a degree in Philosophy from Michigan State University. She first tended bar in two upscale piano bars in Detroit from 1986 to 1992, and has worked in bars and restaurants for almost 20 years. She has been a vegetarian since 1982, at the age of 15, and since discovering raw foods in 2003, she has sought to enthusiastically make the healthiest foods on the planet simpler and more fun for more people. *The Fresh Bartender* is her third recipe book. Her publishing company, Pure Energy Publishing, is based in Seattle, Washington.

"It is often said that before you die your life passes before your eyes.

The Franciscan vineyard in Napa Valley

THE FRESH BARTENDER

... It is in fact true... It's called living." - Terry Pratchett

The Rum Bar at Lake Tahoe

Index

THE FRESH BARTENDER

THE FRESH BARTENDER

Notes

"I think of life itself now as a wonderful play that I've written for myself, and so my purpose is to have the utmost fun playing my part." - Shirley MacLaine

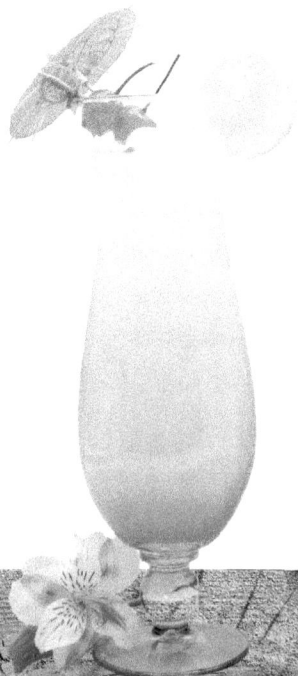

Notes

"People rarely succeed
unless they have fun in
what they are doing."
- Dale Carnegie

Notes

Notes

"There is no pleasure in having nothing to do; the fun is having lots to do and not doing it."
- Mary Wilson Little

www.ingramcontent.com/pod-product-compliance
Lightning Source LLC
LaVergne TN
LVHW021517080426
835509LV00018B/2543